CHOSEN

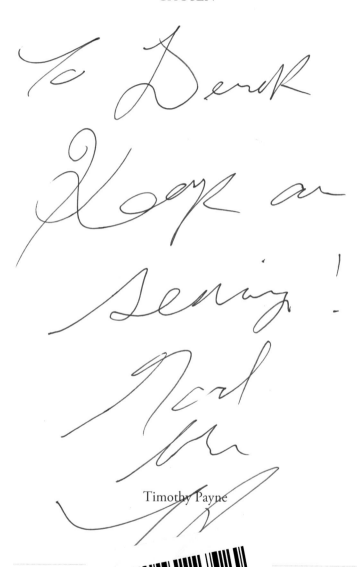

To Derek

Keep on Seeing!

Timothy Payne

D1472375

ISBN-13: 978-1539167907

Contact information for speaking engagements

Chosenleadership.com

timpayne@chosenleadership.com

Contents

Dedication

To the countless non-profit organizations that pay tribute to injured or ill soldiers, your donations compelled me to pay it forward.

To the doctors that saved me through the hundreds of surgeries, blood transfusions and even flat lining multiple times, my hat comes off for you.

To the men and women of the Armed Forces, through your continuous sacrifices, you have inspired me and my decision to push myself to continue serving.

To my family and my dearly beloved brothers, I would crawl through the desert or swim across the ocean just to tell the truth even at the cost of my own life. Thank you all for the support and commitment you've shown, we're all part of a grander design.

Author's Note

The world is a dangerous place full of sorrow and death. On the other end of the spectrum we try to live our lives to the best of our ability and support our loved ones the best we can. We support each other through the tribulations in our world, but how do we individually cope with pain and misery? How are we inspired or comforted in such a crazy world?

The purpose of this book is to give a true testimony to the process of recovery and to give you the tools necessary for defeating all adversity and finally to help others. I never was a man of faith or religion, but after bargaining with God I found myself beginning to believe. After killing the enemy on the field of battle I felt a presence come over me that's almost unexplainable. The presence told me if I lived by the sword then I would die by the sword. I faced the presence head on and immediately started bargaining with the convicting voice and presence. I asked God to take both of my legs in exchange for my life and then, in turn, I would serve him. After losing my legs nearly 24 hours after this encounter, I pushed it away for three years. The presence periodically came back, and it unknowingly revealed a pattern to me. The pattern includes a series of events that have unfolded throughout my military career even stemming from 9/11.

Introduction

The men of the 82nd Airborne are as tough as they come and the events described in the prologue occurred and are articulated in the article "The Last Patrol." On July 5, 2010 Specialist Christopher Moon, 20 years old, a high-school baseball star who had been courted by the Atlanta Braves, chose instead to join the Army. Atop an earthen hesko barrier beside Guard Tower 2 at COP Tynes, he squatted on two ammunition cans and barely moved, like an alligator waiting for prey on a two-hour stretch. He rested his rifle on an iron beam and watched a compound a half mile south. Company outpost Nolan was visible and the Taliban had been attacking both outposts. The insurgents were stashing their weapons and Moon spotted a Taliban fighter with an AK47. The weapon was slung around his back and he jumped up and sped off on a motorcycle. SPC Moon aimed at the fighter center mass and fired his rifle, killing him from over 820 meters; he was as good at sniping as he'd been at baseball. Chris gave up baseball to fight for America. That evening after killing the enemy, Chris spent his night praying for the day and the next day's patrol. "I'm here fighting for my brothers and even to die for them," he thought. He went to sleep confident, knowing the risk and ready for the next day.

The 82nd Paratroopers had been showing the 101st Airborne how to patrol in the area they came to call "The Devils Playground." The risks were so high and constant that sniper support was needed. Sgt. Chris Rush, Moons partner both joined a column of soldiers that snaked out of combat outpost Tynes. They moved east; at a crossroads, the group split. 15 soldiers continued east on Route Red Dog, toward Babur. A dozen others cut south 100 meters and walked along the canal, just inside the tree line. While one group of soldiers moved, the other would cover them, a leapfrog tactic called "bounding overwatch." The split patrol moved forward, in parallel. Ahead, farmers bent at the waist and worked in their grape fields. They'd soon leave for home to wash, pray, and eat. Some saw the patrol and stared and others merely glanced up and then returned working.

A thunderclap rocked the tree line, and the concussion punched their ears and rolled through their chests. Beside them, along the canal, a cloud of smoke and dirt billowed 100 feet into the air, far above the trees, against a cloudless blue sky. "IED! IED! IED!" a soldier barked over the radio. Sergeant Knollinger, leading the element along the road, ran into the field between the road and the canal, toward the explosion, yelling into the hand mike clipped to his vest. "I need a sitrep! I need a sitrep!" Soldiers answered, one by one, save for the two snipers with the patrol. "Viper 4," Knollinger said. "Are you okay? Viper 4!" Sgt. Christopher Rush responded, dazed, his voice slow. "No, I'm not okay." Beside him, his partner, Moon, lay in a crater five feet wide and two feet deep, his legs missing. The triggerman, hidden in the pomegranate orchard, had blown the bomb under Moon, the last man. Gerhart, a leading soldier was 75 feet ahead on the canal trail. He ran back, past a few soldiers who had been knocked to the ground, uninjured. He knelt beside Moon.

Now, his right leg ended above the knee in a thick mass of muscle, skin, and shredded pant leg. His left leg ended in a piece of jagged, shockingly white shinbone. Blood drained into the dirt. Sgt. Gerhart slipped black nylon tourniquets around the stumps. The 101st medic stood nearby and stared at his first battlefield casualty, stunned. "Ah, it hurts so bad," Moon said. Gerhart cranked the tourniquets tight. "You're going to be okay, buddy," he said. Much of Moon's gear had been torn away by the explosion. Soldiers removed the rest. Shrapnel had ripped through his arms, breaking the bones in so many places that his forearms bent and sagged at terrible angles. The medic slid a needle into Moon's arm and started an IV drip of fluids, to replace the lost blood and keep him from slipping into shock. "I'm gonna fucking die," Moon said. Soldiers wrapped bandages around his arms. Bright blood seeped through. "No, man, you're going to be okay," Gerhart said. Moon winced. "I got no legs," he said.

Knollinger called for a medevac, and soldiers lifted Moon onto a stretcher and carried him into a plowed field, away from the crater and any secondary bombs. Back at the combat outpost, a dozen soldiers piled into four armored trucks and sped down Route Red Dog to provide added firepower against follow-on attacks. Moon lay in the sun. The bleeding had stopped. A half-dozen soldiers stood or knelt around him. "Where are the medevac birds?" Moon asked. He faded toward unconsciousness. "Wake up, Moon!" a soldier yelled. "Stay with me!" The trucks arrived, and soon after, the helicopter could be heard on the horizon, beating toward them. "Water," Moon said, his voice a low moan: "Water, please."

Shooting at medevac helicopters had become standard procedure for insurgents, so as the bird approached, low over the fields, soldiers in the gun trucks and on the ground opened up. In a rising racket of machine-gun and rifle fire, bullets shredded trees and kicked up dust in the grape furrows. The helicopter settled into the field and soldiers shielded Moon as dirt swirled over them from the rotor wash. They loaded Moon onto the bird, and his partner, Rush, climbed in beside him. The helicopter lifted and the gunfire diminished. For the next two hours, soldiers scoured the pomegranate orchard, the canal, and a marijuana field for pieces of Moon's equipment, weapon, and legs, all of which had been scattered across a 100-foot radius. They found some of each, and walked home.

For the next week, Moon laid unconscious at Landstuhl Regional Medical Center in Germany, still too unstable for the flight to Walter Reed. Doctors saved his arms, but took more of his left leg, to mid-thigh, and more of his right leg too. His hip, fractured in the blast, had become infected. Moon was strong, the strongest soldier most of his buddies had ever seen, but his body couldn't beat the infection. Specialist Moon Died July 13, 2010.

Dog 13

Fort Drum, New York is the home of the 10th Mountain Infantry Division (Light), and it can be one of the coldest military assignments. Assigned to Dog Company, 1-32 Infantry "Chosin," the rumors circulated nonstop of the coming deployment to Afghanistan and training had been relentless. The rumors were about southern Afghanistan where the Taliban originated. The soldiers of Dog Company just returned from Louisiana, training at JRTC (The Joint Readiness Training Center). The soldiers were sharpening their skills as infantrymen. Skills like firing and maneuvering against enemy forces, combat medical lifesaving, calling for indirect fire such as artillery, airstrikes and mortar systems and a laundry list of other critical skills.

Dog Companies or "D" Companies of light infantry battalions usually hold eighty-five percent of the battalion's firepower. They're composed of anti-tank platoons providing heavier firepower. In the anti-tank platoons, they have wire guided missile systems as well as fifty caliber machine guns and machine fired grenade launchers.

I was assigned to first platoon, third squad, as the Squad Leader; my call sign was "Dog 13," pronounced "dog-one-three." I had the responsibility of making sure all the men were trained and then leading them in war. The company was shifting their fighting capability from vehicle operations to ground operations for patrolling. The rugged terrain was limiting our vehicles, so they weren't an option.

Being assigned to Fort Drum was great because it's three hours from Buffalo. I'm originally from Buffalo, New York, and as a native of Buffalo, we're known for a lot of different things. The most fundamental aspect of Buffalo is that it's close to Niagara Falls, and the Buffalo-style chicken wings are the best in the world! There is also the Buffalo Bills from the National Football League; they fought their way to the super bowl four years in a row and lost. It's like the way I tried out for Special Operations four times and never succeeded, but I digress. President McKinley was also assassinated there. Judging from history, Buffalo is also a thriving city with innovation. Personally, I feel Buffalo is an underdog city of the United States and there's always something to do. How much good can come out of Buffalo? Well, I invite you to come and see.

I traveled from Fort Drum to Buffalo as often as possible. I was visiting family, friends, and my new girlfriend. On January 14, 2011, I hit my eighth year serving the United States Army as an infantryman. I was thinking about the upcoming deployment and how I initially joined the Army back in 2002 for the Army Rangers. I wanted to fight in Afghanistan based on the attacks on the World Trade

Center's on September 11, 2001. I wanted to strike terror with ferocity and uproot their plans; like a crusader.

For me the duty day started at zero four hundred which is four in the morning. I would always make it my point to be first at work. Being at the right place at the right time and in the right uniform was always a top priority. Setting the standard was crucial for mission success. Leaving work always meant being the last of my squad; it's the Squad Leader's job to take care of his soldiers and place their needs above his own. I spent a lot of time getting to know the men of 1st platoon, 3rd squad and they all came from different parts of the United States, even one from a U.S. territory of Saipan.

After the duty day, on my anniversary, I found myself driving home. While driving I notice a large beam cutting through the sky, it looked as if a lens was placed over the sun and a beam of light cut across the sky. Buffalo is where I grew up, went to school and left for the Army exactly eight years prior. I never saw one of these beams before, so this was a first for me. I took a picture, and the first thing I did after arriving home was to research the phenomenon (Luke 21:25). It was labeled a sundog, but I never heard or seen one before. I thought it was weird. I have always been interested in science, astronomy and how everything works in the universe. I had been all over the world and seen lots of different things, but this was new. I chalked it up as something new and went about my business spending time with family and researching the war in Afghanistan.

The Last Patrol

Announcements flowed through the unit confirming where we would be going to in Afghanistan. Upon the notification, all the Squad Leaders were ordered to the battalion conference room to hear a briefing about our combat area. The Battalion command team wanted to speak only to the squad leaders. This was because we would be leading the patrols in combat. We would have fire teams, forward observers, medics, machine gun and mortar teams, the Afghanistan National Army (ANA) and interpreters. The amount of responsibility was immense for us and a lot of lives were in our hands.

Lieutenant Colonial (LTC) Mintz and Command Sergeant Major (CSM) Horny briefed all the Squad Leaders. We were instructed to read "The Last Patrol," an article that appeared in the Atlantic Journal just four months prior to the meeting. It was written by Brian Mockenhaupt and detailed his experience in Afghanistan.

It described our area of operation in Southern Afghanistan known as the Arghandab River Valley. The story of the last patrol was about the events of their final patrol and what transpired with 2nd Platoon, Charlie Company 2-508 PIR Parachute Infantry Regiment (PIR), 82nd Airborne Division and the 1-320 Field Artillery, 101st Airborne Division. While reading, I took notice of how I originally started in the 3-325 Airborne Infantry Regiment (AIR), 82nd Airborne Division, but after my second deployment we changed names and became the 2-508 PIR. This article was composed after I left the Airborne. I was assigned to them from August 2003 until October 2005.

The first unit I belonged to was losing half of their men, and they labeled Arghandab the "The Devils

Playground." Throughout the article, the men of 2 Charlie (2-508) took horrendous casualties. Nearly every time they would go on patrol a frightening situation would arise. It was surreal to read about such losses.

Their replacements were from the artillery, not infantry. They had big shoes to fill in the deadliest place in Afghanistan. They had a mission to push further into Taliban territory, but they were unfamiliar with the area. The leadership of the 82nd wanted a positive handoff showing the 101st how to patrol and more importantly, what not to do. This was their final patrol, and they would be going deeper into Taliban territory. They knew pushing deeper would mean losses and with half the men of Two Charlie shot up, blown up or killed, tensions were high.

The patrol left late due to communication issues and during the walk the enemy started harassing the patrol with small arms fire. They were getting pinned down as they made their way deeper into enemy territory. With the new soldiers not acclimated to the heat, many started becoming heat casualties. After being pinned down, the men of 2 Charlie called in helicopter gunships to break up the attack. After so long, the paratroopers had to fight their way back, displaying multiple acts of valor. The terrain was harsh with visibility very low; you could only see 90 feet in front of you due to the foliage. Fighting through the farm fields and grape rows is like playing a chess game with improvised explosive devices and bullets. The men made it back to their compound while under attack. More than half of the new soldiers were suffering from heat exhaustion and were severely dehydrated. The heat will kill you fast. It starts with dehydration, followed by muscle cramps and then heat stroke. Your brain literally cooks as the core temperature soars.

While finishing the patrol, medical evacuations were called as well as resupplying water and ammunition. The leaders were also butting heads about what should be done. Airstrikes were delayed and then called in to keep the enemy back. Finally, the men came back finishing their patrol hugging each other, thankful they didn't have to go back after that patrol.

Later, the 101st Airborne Division lost many soldiers, and the losses were soaring the same as the 82nd Airborne Division. It takes hard lessons learned to know what to do and what not to do in "The Devils Playground."

After reading the article and considering my job as a squad leader, I knew I was going to lose men and most likely get killed. We were tasked with destroying the enemy who were oppressing the local Afghanis and denying them the freedom to move in our area. I would be in the middle of the action the whole time. Reading the words "devils playground" multiple times caused me to pause and pray for the first time saying, "God, if you're really out there, and one of us has to go, then just kill me instead of my men. I don't want live with survivors' guilt!"

I thought about all my friends living with survivors' guilt and how I didn't want it. I couldn't stand the fact of losing just one, so I decided to work hard to prepare myself for the fight that I knew would come. I read a book called "War" by Sebastian Junger, and it motivated me to prepare even more. There is also the documentary film on the book called "Restrepo." I watched the film and the 173rd Airborne Division was the center point. I just left that unit prior to arriving to Fort Drum. I needed as much knowledge as possible men are counting on us to make the right decisions. I had no other choice but to give one hundred percent of myself and then some more if possible.

Weeks before the deployment, many classes were conducted including the possibility of not returning home. Training ranges consisting of weapon marksmanship and demolitions were carried out weekly. We learned how to use high explosives to destroy IEDs. We were constantly fine-tuning our skills as infantrymen.

Later we received the most advanced equipment; lighter body armor, advance medical kits, tourniquets, newer gloves, heavy, medium and light assault packs, newer boots and new combat uniforms. We were issued the best the Army could offer, and without hesitation, I started buying extra supplies. I was spending thousands of dollars on equipment for my men. I wanted them to have the gear I wanted and to me it made sense. I was purchasing better gloves, better eye protection, multipurpose tools and other supplies. The top priority was placing their needs above my own as is articulated in the Creed of Noncommissioned Officers (NCO Creed).

I packed up my apartment and started moving all my personal belongings back to Buffalo. I was preparing for the worse and kept the truth from my family. I was telling them I could save more money not paying for rent, so it made sense.

.

A few days later while working in the Platoon Sergeants office, the official orders for Afghanistan arrived and at the same time I also received official orders for special operations! It was a position I applied for 6 months ago before moving from Italy. I worked for a year and a half straight to submit the application. It read: *Congratulations SSG Timothy Payne for being selected for Special Operations, with a class date of 22 July 2012.*

So there I was in February 2011 looking at my orders for Afghanistan in one hand and Special Forces in the other. I originally joined the Army to fight in Afghanistan and to be a special operator. All my goals were coming to fruition after 7 years of service, and all I needed now was to survive a year in the Devils Playground and then continue to train for a possible covert position with the Special Forces.

Leadership

Special Operations was the only force I wanted to fight with. It was at the top of my list regarding personal goals for a fulfilling career. It takes a lot of training and discipline to achieve such goals, and the selection process is rigorous. I applied four times since joining the Army, but was always disappointed because of either medical drops or official orders from the Army.

Since I previously wasn't selected for Special Forces, I applied for civil affairs. This request was answered six months after submission. I wasn't surprised with the selection orders because I was more than qualified, but out of the four times applying things hadn't changed. I thought "Murphy" hated me and was out to get me. Murphy is that Army dupe that says whatever can go wrong will go wrong. It seemed I either received orders or was injured days before changing my Army job.

My first attempt for elite forces was with the Army Rangers right after Infantry school. I was 20 years old at the time and had to complete airborne training as a prerequisite, so I made sure Rangers was in my signing contract; I wouldn't join unless it was so. I arrived at the 75th Ranger Regiment, and the program was designed to be three weeks of pre-Ranger training and then the two-week "Ranger Indoctrination Program" (RIP) would follow.

Our class arrived at the 75th Ranger Regiment five weeks before the start date. There weren't any classes being conducted due to the annual Ranger Rendezvous hosted by 3rd Ranger Battalion and then Independence Day weekend. The rendezvous is a tradition bringing the Ranger Regiment together for change of command and other events. The

majority of the Rangers just arrived back from deployment, so
they were currently on leave. The place felt like a ghost town.
Our pre-Ranger instructors were there and they brutally
trained us from the first day we arrived. The course was
extended by an additional three weeks due to Independence
Day.

After grueling physical fitness (PT) sessions and
relentless mind games, we were finally beginning to learn
Ranger standards. Five weeks into training, one instructor
noticed me limping after an eight-mile run. He yelled out at
me, telling me to go see a medic. I was told that after eight
straight months of continuous training and five weeks with
the Rangers, I sustained severe stress fractures on my
shinbones. I was immediately dropped from the program.

I was reassigned to the 82nd Airborne Division where
I went to Delta Company, 3-325th Airborne Infantry

Regiment or the "The Blue Falcons" where I deployed for the initial push in support of Operation Iraqi Freedom. After the first deployment, I earned the coveted Expert Infantryman's Badge, and then I deployed again for a second tour back to Baghdad, Iraq.

After the second deployment, I submitted a Special Forces application after attending a briefing. The briefing consisted of all the training that would be required and described the intense commitment we would need. The Special Operations command always needs highly motivated soldiers, and all who are interested can sign a waiver locking them in for official orders. I liked what I heard about the training and being part of something bigger than myself. The recruiter told everyone in the briefing to discuss our decisions with our families over the weekend. I was so eager and I didn't have a wife or children to talk it over with, so I raised my hand and stated I wanted to sign the orders now. The Special Forces Recruiter said, "If you want to be Special

Forces, then the first rule was to follow orders and come back Monday." I took his advice, and as soon as Monday came along, I told my Section Leader what my plan was. That is when I learned that I just received orders that morning for Army Recruiting. So, the very same day I was trying to do something bigger than myself I received orders for Army recruiting.

Recruiting was one of the toughest jobs I had. I was an expert infantryman and paratrooper, not a pencil pushing recruiter! Although I disliked the idea of recruiting, I did not want to fail this assignment. If I wanted to be elite, I better adapt and overcome. The Special Forces recruiter told me that recruiting had a higher priority and that I better stick it out and come back three years later.

During this tough transition in the Army, I went from being in the infantry to recruiting. If it weren't for the

Army values dictating my actions and lifestyle, I wouldn't have been able to complete the job like I did. The Army values are represented by the acronym LDRSHIP (Loyalty, duty, respect, selfless-service, honor, integrity and personal courage) and it's the duty of every person to live according to these values. I worked physically and mentally based on these values and this system had been a part of my work ethic since I was a private during basic training. If I lived by these values, that meant I would be doing the right thing always. I'm not perfect, but if I make the right decision during stressful situations, I would be fine.

Recruiting wasn't easy; it took over a year to learn the new job and as a result. Fortunately, during fiscal year 2007, I was among the top ten percent of all recruiters in the state of New York. I was even meritoriously promoted from Sergeant to Staff Sergeant during that time. It was a constant challenge in this changing world, and had to adapt mentally and overcome it by practicing those LDRSHIP values. Leadership is described as the process of giving purpose, direction, and motivation to achieve a goal.

My first recruiting boss went to the psych ward, and he left our station shortly afterward. We had fill-in station commanders for a time until the second station commander arrived. Sergeant First Class (SFC) Barnes was a former paratrooper who helped guide me during my second year; I owe a lot of my success to him and then others who helped me along the way. During my third year (after promotion), I attended two leadership schools. I participated in the Warrior Leadership Course and then the Advanced Leadership Course. While attending the schools, I was reminded of my life in the infantry and the hard learned skills I was beginning to loose because of my time away. I decided to brush up on infantry standards and procedures, and I suddenly realized how much I missed the infantry.

After coming back from school, I was motivated for my third and final year of recruiting, but my third station commander turned out to be toxic. A toxic commander is extremely difficult to work with, and he began micromanaging my every move directly after school. He was trying to control my work day by dictating my routine.

I was written up for missing phone calls and yelled at for not conducting briefings with him every hour over applicants. I finally pushed back when he started asking me to falsify documents for unqualified applicants. He was violating the Army Values, so I stood my ground on the basis of integrity and doing what's right regardless of the outcome. If I falsified documents and was caught, then I'd lose my career, face jail time or lose rank and pay. I kept my mouth shut and tried staying under the radar with all the work place abuse.

More verbal altercations between us resulted as he harassed me more and more. Finally, one day after prospecting for applicants, I arrived at the Recruiting Center. As I was walking inside he started gnashing his teeth at me for something ridiculous, "Payne, get in here!" He shouted from his office. I couldn't take the abuse any more. I stormed straight in his office as he yelled at me. I closed the door quickly and turned my attention sharply to him. I locked enraged eyes on him as he threw my inch thick counseling packet on the desk. He started explaining to me that he was going to demote me for not signing anyone in the army. I had a better idea telling him my perceptions on respect.

I said, "As a Noncommissioned officer and leader in the United States Army, I earned my rank through knowledge and execution, based on my decision making process and conduct. I earned my rank and title just as you have, so I deserve the same respect I'm giving you. Treat me like a man or hit me and give me an excuse!"

He backed off fast, as his demeanor changed, he reached for the phone and called the company 1st Sergeant (1SG) who oversees all training and personnel. He ordered me to go and see him, so I left and drove to the Company Station. After making the fifty-mile trip north to Syracuse, I explained to him what was going on from the beginning. The First Sergeant told me I could move to a different recruiting station where I could relax for three months since I would be leaving soon. I was leaving recruiting after 3 years of craziness and going to Vicenza, Italy. I went from being one of the best recruiters to the worst because of toxic leadership.

My younger brother was the second person I had signed up for the Army, and he is a paratrooper like myself. He was also in the 173rd Airborne Division, the same place I was going to in Italy. It was exciting to be stationed with my sibling in an entirely different country. I arrived in Italy on October of 2008, and this time I went straight to the Special

Forces recruiter and signed my waiver the same day getting there.

I left for training January 2009 and started Special Force's Assessment and Selection course (SFAS) at Fort Bragg North Carolina. Two days before completing the course I sustained injuries to my right knee and right my hip. The Discovery Channel was there filming the show "Two Weeks in Hell" and my roster number was 155, they caught the injury and interviewed me right there on the spot. Once again, I became another medical drop and felt like "Murphy" was still out to get me.

After arriving back to my unit, I was reassigned to Personnel Recovery Operations under the Southern European Task Force or SETAF. After completing my training, I started training physically and mentally for another position. I was working with senior Special Forces operators and told them my story. The Master Sergeant said with my background in recruiting and infantry, I should be working in civil affairs. It sounded fascinating, but also required a lot more testing.

I completed my testing and submitted my application a little over year later. I retook the Armed Service Vocational Aptitude Battery for the third time and received a 78 on the test. The test measures your ability for training and learning a new skill set. The qualifying score to join the Army is a 32, and the first time I took the test I scored a 44, which is the national average.

I wanted to be a Ranger, but I needed at least a 50 on the test. I told my recruiter back in 2001 that I would not join anything unless I had a Ranger contract, so for a year I went and paid for tutoring at the Huntington Learning Center. I took the test again six months later and scored a 54. I signed my Ranger Contract October 2002 just a few days before my mom's Birthday. I had a training date January 14, 2003 and just turned 20 years old (Numbers 1:3), once again my intention was rooted to 9/11.

So here I am, seven years in the Army and finally scoring a 78 on the ASVAB test and preparing to take the Defense Language Aptitude Battery as the final requirement for Civil Affairs. This test assesses your ability to learn a new language. I took it three times like the ASVAB and finally scored an 85, which is the minimum score required to pass. Finally, I was able to submit my packet for Civil Affairs pursuing a covert job working abroad in different countries with Special Forces teams, almost like a precursor to a CIA operative. I submitted my packet, but on the same day I was notified that I was leaving for a new assignment at Fort Drum, New York. At this point in time, I figured someone was out to get me. If it wasn't an injury, it was orders.

The Devil's Playground

I remember watching the news about the Fukushima earthquake (Mark 13:8) just days before our deployment. To date, it's been the biggest nuclear disaster in history. The entire Pacific Ocean had been irradiated, killing the marine life (Revelation 8:6). The carcasses of dead marine animals have been washing up on shores since the initial fallout. While watching the tsunami take out part of Japan, I thought about how the 82nd went and helped in the aftermath of Hurricane Katrina in 2005. Maybe the unit would send us to Japan rather Afghanistan, wishful thinking.

All the packing was completed, and the rear detachment was coordinating all transportation to the airports. The men from Dog Company, 1-32nd Infantry "Chosin" departed to Afghanistan in mid-March 2011. It was the onset of a new year according to the Holy Scriptures

(Leviticus 23:5). We were welcomed with rocket attacks on KAF (Kandahar Airfield), the base was being hit by Chinese made rockets that would send eight metallic boomerangs in every direction, slicing through body parts. That week a female soldier had lost both her legs in the attack.

We haven't arrived at our area of operation yet, so we were conducting IED detection course and area briefings regarding the enemy forces. After two short weeks, our unit pushed out to "The Devils Playground" by Chinook helicopters. It was the beginning of April, and the 101st Airborne had sustained horrific casualties; they stressed the importance of attention to detail. They led combat patrols just as the 82nd had done the year prior, giving us much needed familiarization. The terrain was more than challenging, and maneuvering through the lush grape orchards, poppy farms and marijuana fields made for a surreal experience.

The terrain was rough and we always took the path of most resistance, meaning we would climb ten feet walls rather than walking through a break in the wall. That is where the Taliban would usually place IED's. The whole area was littered with these makeshift bombs. They would range in weight from a couple of pounds to 1,500 pounds. The "Screaming Eagles" (101st Airborne Division) told us about the hard lessons they learned from friends they lost. They would put fear in us to keep us on edge. So many stories were shared about the brave men and woman that died there. They helped us acculturate for two weeks before relocating to RC-East (Regional Command Eastern Afghanistan) before their return to the United States.

After the 101st Airborne left, our platoon was up for patrol. First squad went out and a good man was injured on that patrol. Fitz stepped on a land mine that blew off his right leg at the knee. After that incident, the platoon sergeant gathered all the men in the squad leaders' tent and briefed all of us about the loss. Fitz was considered the brains of the lower enlisted soldiers. No one thought he would get injured, but then again this is war. War doesn't show favoritism to anyone. The men took the loss hard and as a result, my squad went out to help the patrol. During my walk out, one of my soldiers became a heat casualty. Irving was a rifleman in my squad, and he passed-out while patrolling. It was over 100 degrees outside and our equipment weighed about hundred of pounds. Just weeks before the patrol, I stressed to the soldiers to hydrate and drink water. A lot of men were drinking sodas that would dehydrate you faster. Doc Garcia started an IV for Irving giving him replacement fluids that he lost. This was just the beginning of our deployment, and we could see how things would unfold from here.

After four months of fighting at Company Outpost Zharif Khel, all squads took losses and we were deemed combat ineffective as of July 1. Soldiers either were shot, blown up or killed. Our unit policy was to have a continuous presence in enemy territory. We were always out patrolling to deny the enemy the freedom to move throughout the area. Multiple combat engagements were fought and our company was undermanned. We were losing our tempo as casualty's soared. We became combat ineffective in the beginning of the Taliban's primary summer fighting season.

The day prior to July 1, my squad fought through two near ambushes, which resulted in zero casualties. It was literally a miracle. It was like the scene from the movie *Pulp Fiction* when two assassins where ambushed by a man hiding in the bathroom. Our mission was to meet an informant in a specific village and as we approach the village the road curved. Private First Class Barnett was walking with the team up front when a hidden bomb exploded under his right foot. The ambush cooked off with bullets flying directly at that team. The entire group dropped to the ground. Specialist Merritt was the point man carrying the minesweeper. Three other soldiers, Barnett, Stetler and Irving, supported the point man.

We launched 40-millimeter grenades against the enemy to the north with the new M320 grenade launcher just 15 meters away from where Taliban fighter's hid behind a tiny bridge firing PKM machineguns. In a matter of seconds, the team achieved fire superiority. While they were laying down suppressive fire, I saw Taliban forces in their position directly to my front, which was to the east. They were firing directly at the rest of my squad and me. We were hit with an L-Shaped ambush. It looked as if the whole Alpha team was blown up. In this type of attack there is no other place to go. If you flee, the men die. If you stay in the kill zone, you die. The rest of the squad, Afghan National Army forces and myself assaulted directly towards the enemy. As we rushed through gunfire, we used our weapons to create a wall of bullets and grenades flying towards the enemy. The enemy fled from the area very quickly. We took cover and set up a perimeter on the road while sending a report to our headquarters. The report disclosed the amount of ammunition expended and our required resupply, what casualties (if any) and any equipment that was damaged or destroyed during the incident. Merritt, who was holding the minesweeper, felt his foot sink in the sand. He stepped on an IED.

He felt a click and heard a creak like a rusty spring. He looked to me franticly and said "Sarge!!! I think I'm stepping on an IED." I looked at him while waiting for the report and said, "Well, get off it." We scanned the area with the mine detector and discovered it was a bomb. We blew it up in place with explosives. Remarkably, no one was hurt during the incident. Stetler was wounded with a miner scrape on his shoulder, everyone had enough ammunition and there was no damage to our equipment. I couldn't believe how lucky we were. Even Barnett nothing wrong, we should have been killed or lost a few men from the attack.

After gaining our senses from the intense attack, we decided to set up a traffic control point right outside the town. There was two hours left on our patrol, and we intended to stay there monitoring the village and people. It was the same area where most the attacks were coming from.

After interrogating villagers, we were unable to find our known informant. We thought we were set up. We left the village and took positions north of the town in a defensive posture. On a bending road, I had one team cover the west and the other watch the north. The Afghan army was intermingled with command section and machine gun team in the middle. We had enough cover and concealment. So, if anyone came into our area, they would have been surrounded by a wall of fire. We all had enough excitement for the day. Only two hours remained on our patrol, and we were ready to return to our combat outpost.

As we were about to return to base, two motorcycles approached the control point. A soldier Sablan, who we called

"Coconut," went to search the men. While he was walking toward them, the two men fled and the watching Taliban fighters revealed their hiding position behind a wall some forty feet away. They attacked us.

We were spread apart on an L-shaped road with a team on each end. The Command team was in the center, behind a building by two ditches running parallel to the road in the center. When the attack began, machine gun fire was directed at my position. I jumped behind a soldier named Barlow, observing his sector of fire. He was hammering the enemy with machine gun fire, sending powerful .308 caliber rounds directly at the Talibs. That machine gun was a twenty-five-pound powerhouse of destruction capable of exploding body parts on contact. I couldn't get a good view of the battle, so I leapt into the ditch and crawled to the center of the road, also the center of the battle space. I sprang up and saw Barnett firing grenades at the enemy. I ran up to him while observing to the west and saw the other team returning suppressive fire. I ran next to Barnett while he was exposed to the enemy's line of sight and yelled at him to get behind the tree next to him.

I looked over toward the north and saw Irving and Stetler returning fire. I immediately saw the team had good cover while returning fire. I ran across the road through enemy gunfire to link up with Stetler and Irving. Sergeant Smerbeck, the platoon sergeant, was at the center of the location, still by the building coordinating immediate mortar suppression with our company fires. He was trying to get high explosive mortars to fall on the enemy. Stetler and Irving had adrenaline pumping through their veins as they were screaming and shouting in excitement. They were firing relentlessly. I reached their spot and jumped into the ditch line on the road. The fire from the enemy position started to die down when I collected both of them and the three of us maneuvered north and directly west, flanking the enemy's position behind the wall. The shooting was over but we didn't know if they were waiting for us. I threw an M67 fragmentation grenade into their position to clear out the enemy. "Cooking off" a hand grenade is intense. Imagine holding a metal ball full of explosives that will blow up in five seconds. I counted to two and lobbed the grenade over the wall. As soon as it exploded, I led the men through and cleared the area. Soon after, I was ordered back to base.

We arrived back safely and conducted a review of the patrol. I kept thinking about how lucky that none of us were killed. Stetler was scratched on his right shoulder from shrapnel and Barnett did have a small shrapnel wound from the bomb he stepped on. He also had bullet holes in a new uniform he wore, he was pissed. Stetler was the only one listed as a combat injury. Since he was injured, so submitted his name for the Purple Heart award. Years later would I find out Barnett had been injured during the attack as well. It was literally a miracle that no one was killed. After our patrol review, I was left thinking about how easily we could have of lost one of our teams in the attack.

Combat Ineffective

The next morning, third platoon rotated for patrol and PFC Pack just arrived from leave. It was his first time out again. He was blown up on that patrol and lost his leg above the knee. He was evacuated immediately. Soon after, third platoon was in a firefight. Then our base started taking fire as well. The Talibs at this point were taking the fight to where we slept as well as the patrolling squads. They were hitting us with more sophisticated attacks.

My squad was guarding the eastern wall of the outpost during these attacks. While mounting the wall and returning fire, soldiers to my left were ducking behind the hesco wall for cover. A hesco wall is nothing more than a giant basket filled with dirt and then blocked together like Legos. I was yelling to scan for the enemy and return fire. To my right, my machine gunner Brooks yelled at me that he needed more ammo. I told him to go get the ammo while I continued scanning for enemy positions using the scope attached to my carbine. Bullets hissed by my head. I was looking for movement on the horizon, and I found some quickly. I saw a silhouette of a man bobbing up and down. I thought he was hiding behind a tree, but I saw an AK47. He was popping up, firing at us, and then hiding again. Once I identified him, my infantry training kicked in. I steadied my position, controlled my breathing, aimed and prepared to squeeze the trigger. "One shot, one kill," as we say.

All this transpired in a matter of seconds. I was getting ready to shoot this man when I glanced over and saw Brooks' unmanned machine gun with a hundred round belt of ammunition. I looked at my rifle and looked back at the SAW; I looked back at my rifle and then again at the SAW. I put my rifle down, grabbed the machine gun, deployed the bipod, charged the weapon and adjusted my site picture at the base of the enemy target.

I knew it took a matter of milliseconds for the rounds to be fired and travel the 300 meters to hit the target, accounting for the muzzle drift traveling up towards the right. I waited for the enemy to start moving back up and before he could get into his firing position. I yelled out the distance, direction and description of the combatant known as the 3 D's and started firing. Barlow heard me call out the information and he engaged at the same time. I watched this man take hits from the SAW and the M240 Bravo. I watched his body explode to pieces by the .308 rounds and the 5.56mm rounds. This was the first person I shot and killed.

I thought to myself, "Wow, I just killed that guy. Okay, I'm doing my job."

At the same time after shooting this man, I felt a presence come over me that I never felt before. It gave me chills and made my hair stand straight up all over my body despite the 100 degree heat. I heard a voice in my head say, "If you live by the sword, you die by the sword" (Matthew 26:52).

I didn't know what it was, but at the same time I was also wondering, "Why am I thinking about this? I'm doing my job!" Without time to reflect there was a reply.

"It doesn't matter. You killed your fellow man, therefore you're going to pay for what you've done." Instantly fear came over me, I asked, "Is this God?"

And the reply was, "Yes."

I instantly felt as if I had been late to work for the last time and would be fired. I immediately bargained with the presence: "Don't Kill me, shoot me instead."

"No."

"Okay, take one of my legs!"

The response was, "No."

"Okay, forget this. I'm done with you," and I started to ignore the presence and voice.

I did everything I could to ignore the voice. The firefight was over and third platoon was still out finishing their fight. They fought through it, and the next squad would be going out in a few hours.

I went to the gym at the outpost to try to clear my head, but the voice was like a broken record. I tried pushing it away by working out. Two hours went by, and it never left. After the gym, I went to the Internet café and talked to my family and friends about the deployment. In a couple of hours, third platoon came back and went back out again for the night. During the early evening one of the Soldiers came into the Internet tent. He was distraught and announced that third platoon was hit with two casualties, Bryan and Waters. PFC James Waters was killed instantly from an IED and

Bryan lost three of his limbs on July 1st. The next announcement was third platoon was coming back. According to protocol, the café was shut down until the Waters family could be notified. Everyone was shocked and sadness flowed through Dog Company.

Our unit had become combat ineffective after just four months in the "Devil's Playground." I felt terrible for the guys we just lost and at the same time I was selfish to be thankful I hadn't lost any men. The company sustained casualties in all squads, apart from mine. Although I was almost killed along with my guys just the day prior, I couldn't believe how lucky we were. If we lost any more soldiers, we wouldn't be able to cover all the guard positions.

Finally at the end of the night, while playing Angry Birds in my tent, but that voice in my head came back and would not leave me alone. It repeated itself over and over again, it was frustrating and I couldn't fall asleep. I put my IPOD down and said, "Okay! Please don't kill me. I'll do whatever you want! I'll read your word; I'll spread your word. Take both of my legs, I'll do whatever you want, but please don't kill me!" (Numbers 21:2-3). Nothing but silence came after, and I fell asleep. I only said those things because I was thinking how I yelled at Duncan the day prior for reading the bible before patrol. I thought God was real pissed at me and this was really unexplainable.

The next day Sgt. Smerbeck had scheduled a briefing on the new operation template for the remainder of the deployment. It sounded like we were going to be sitting in vehicles on access roads from here on out. By lunchtime, the Company Command team ordered a meeting with the ANA. They were figuring out the plan, and the ANA wanted to have a goat for lunch. I never saw a goat slaughtered before, and I was eager to watch so I grabbed my camera and ran over to video the slaughter. Before the ANA started slicing away at the goat's throat, they said a prayer (Leviticus 16). The amount of blood coming out was unreal, and I was filming the whole scene.

Directly after the slaying, SFC Smerbeck approached me and told that the patrols were officially ending, however there was one last patrol left at the location where I killed the Talib the day prior. It was considered the last patrol, and because I hadn't lost any soldiers, I was chosen. The plan was to destroy the enemy fighting position using our old rockets and explosives. We would fire them, then clear it out with demolitions. The plan was simple and we had over-watch protection from outpost.

July 3

The next morning, July 3, 2011, we left the outpost around 9am, making our way out through the entrance control point at the west gate and skirting the southern wall. We had all the protection we needed as we approached our vantage point just east of the south tower. Our snipers were with us. So we started firing our rockets to destroy the enemy position, but there was no damage to the position. The Taliban heard the rockets being fired and were trying to determine if we stepped on one of their IED's. Knowing Taliban fighters were in the area, our platoon leadership decided to set up a counter-ambush about fifty meters north. I argued against this at the last minute, thinking the squad's fighting capability would be diminished. If we split the squad like the leadership intended, we would be taking away from our ability to maneuver. My argument was ruled out, and I followed orders.

I took Merritt, who had the minesweeper, Barnett with the SAW and a sniper from the Scout platoon. I told Barnett and Merritt to set up an anti-personnel mine to cover the east of our position while we watched our guys from the north to the south. Directly north behind our designated spot, there was a ten-foot wall and the guard towers could overwatch what was out of sight. We were covered from all directions, but we still needed to set up the anti-personnel claymore mine. This device is a directional anti-personnel mine containing 700 ball bearings. When it is fired, it sends those ball bearings in a one-hundred-and-eighty-degree cone, shredding everything for over 100 meters. The mine was covering our eastern flank.

While moving into position, Merritt walked with the minesweeper, marking the cleared path with baby powder while Barnett and I followed. I told the sniper to cover us. We walked about fifteen meters and placed the claymore in a well-hidden position. I told Merritt and Barnett to camouflage the mine while I unreeled the spool of wire back to the sniper position. The mine is detonated by an electric firing mechanism that sends an electrical charge to ignite the explosives. As soon as I moved back to the sniper, I ask if everything was prepared and he gave me the thumbs up and nodded. I walked back to Merritt and Barnett while camouflaging the wire using dirt and brush from the ground. I took one step off the cleared path to grab some more brush when the presence I felt just the other day came charging right at and me saying, "Get ready!"

I had no idea what to make of it, but a gut wrenching feeling came over me as I looked at the ground. I thought to myself, "what the hell?" And then BOOM! A massive bomb exploded directly in front of me. I just realized that I had been blown up as my two-hundred-and forty-five-pound body went flying through the air and trees.

Denial shot through my mind like a lightning bolt and my thoughts raced like speeding bullets: "I had a good life, I traveled the world, and I'm dying for my men, this makes sense." "Charge it," my squad motto, I'm thought to myself. Everything was making sense because I thought I was dying for my men (John 15:13). I accepted my death and felt myself slipping away.

Merritt and Barnett were camouflaging the claymore when the IED went off. They were shaken up, and filled with adrenaline they ran to my aid. They initially mistook the bomb for the claymore mine. They immediately picked themselves up and rushed towards my position. I remember grunting in disbelief about how mangled I was. I asked Merritt, "How bad is it?" He replied, "Both your legs are gone below the knees."

The next thing I asked was if my manhood was still there, he said they could fix it. My two saviors put tourniquets on all my limbs, wrapped up my manhood and were feverishly trying to stabilize me. My left forearm looked like a scorched chicken wing with a huge bite out of it. I could see through my arm, and the bones were completely exposed. The tendons and muscle tissue was dangling from the palm to my elbow. It was so surreal. I thought, "That doesn't look right." I glanced at my right arm as I spit dirt and debris out of my mouth. It wasn't as bad, just some holes through my forearm. My pelvis separated itself and my lower abdomen was ripped open. I was suffering from arterial bleeding. Blood squirted out of my body at a rapid rate like a water jug tipped on its side. I could see my right leg and the strands of muscle hanging from what used to be my right knee. I couldn't see my left leg because it was blown wide open from the knee up.

Merritt secured all the bandages and tightened all tourniquets as hard as he could. Barnett was on the radio reporting the situation because the Platoon Sergeant thought we had fired the claymore mine on the enemy. He reported, "Dog 13 is down, Dog 13 is down!" There was still blood coming out of my abdomen. Merritt tried shoving his hand inside of me, but his gloves were too bulky. He struggled to pull his gloves off, his grip slipping because of the blood that covered his body. Mike had no other choice but to use his teeth to pull them off finger by finger. Once the gloves were off, he stuck his hand inside my warm abdomen and clamped the pulsating artery. The rest of the men came running to my aid to further stabilize me despite having to traverse terrain that wasn't cleared. When they finally reached me, they opened the collapsible litter.

The nine-line medevac was called over the radio, and luckily there were helicopters passing through the area intercepting the calls. The men had to pick me up causing my pelvis to shift abnormally. The pain shot through me like a wakeup call. It was one of the most painful things I've felt in my life. The SFC Smerbeck felt responsible and was apologizing to me as I was evacuated. I told him to forget about it.

Our medic, Coconut, who was an EMT before joining the army, checked me over because Merritt and Barnett needed a break. Merritt was drenched in my blood, and the platoon sergeant was yelling at him, "Are you hit?" He wasn't, but with the amount of blood covering him, you would think otherwise. Doc Smiraldi, who was also there, helped as well and told another soldier to jam gauze in my wounds. The men bandaged me up and stripped my uniform and equipment off. My ammo pouches and gear had been completely annihilated. At that point, they were ready to carry me to the landing zone.

On the way to the landing zone where the medevac chopper would land, the men had to carry me across and down an eight-foot drop into a ditch. Being conscious, I yelled at them "Please, Don't drop me!" Not only did I get blown up, I was worried that my guys would drop me in this ditch. They didn't drop me; rather, they ran to the landing site carrying me and waited. Two more soldiers from the platoon, Cobb and Brooks also helped carry what was left of me. During the wait for the chopper, Sgt. Smerbeck grabbed my right hand and told me he was sorry about the mission. I said to him, "Who cares man, it's all good." I was coherent. So, the guys encouraged me to keep talking to them.

"What the hell do you want me to say? I'm sorry I got blown up." I said aloud to everyone. Moments later, to appease the men, the first thing I thought to do was sing a song, so I sang *She'll be coming around the mountain*. I sang as loud as I could. I don't know if any of them were laughing but in my mind, I wanted them at ease.

The Blackhawk helicopter picked me up, and I was taken to Kandahar Airfield. The flight medic checked all my wounds and wanted to start an intravenous infusion, but with the tourniquets on my limbs (eight in all) it would not be possible. Instead, he punched an interosseous infusion directly into my sternum by hovering over me and using his body weight to force the device into me. It felt like a major punch to the chest. I watched him hook the tube to the bag of fluids that began draining into me in a matter of seconds. My body was absorbing everything quickly because I lost a lot of blood. When the Blackhawk helicopter finally landed and the door slid open, I was greeted by the nurses. I was rushed to the emergency room and along the way, I saw the prettiest nurses as they looked at my blown up naked body. I told them, "Please don't look at me." I thought the last thing I wanted would be for these beautiful nurses to look down at a blown up manhood.

I was taken to the operating room, and the doctors asked me, "Do you know what happened to you?" I told them yes and described my injury to them: "My name is Staff Sergeant Timothy Payne, I was blown up in Kandahar 0930 July 3rd 2011. What else do you want me to say?" I didn't know what else to say to them, but without thinking the Doctor told me they were going to put me out and take care of me. I started yelling at them, "Put me out! Put me out! Put me out!" Everything went black.

Two Weeks in Hell

Part I – Catacombs

I felt myself waking up in a cool damp setting, and before opening my eyes I could feel moisture between my fingers. The smell of morning dew filled my nostrils before I even opened my eyes. When I opened my eyes, I wondered where I was. It was a dark, massive catacomb. I looked down a long cavern that angled downward with massive pillars fifty to sixty feet apart. And on each column, a lantern gave just enough light to reveal the structure. Everything was pitch black and spooky. I turned my head to look in the other direction and the ground started moving. Rocks and boulders erupted out of the ground and began to form a shape of a massive beast twice my size. Terror crawled up my spine and the hairs all over my body were sticking straight up. The creature had red glowing and pulsating eyes. As soon as I stood up, it locked onto my movement, snarled at me like a ravaging wolf and bolted right towards me. I could only see its massive silhouette as it dashed towards me from twenty or thirty feet away.

I sprang up and ran as fast I could, not looking back. It screeched at me with ferocity as I scurried away. I could see the lanterns zipping by as I ran down this spiral shaped cavern. What I noticed beyond the pillars was a massive drop off like a cliff. There was no other place to go. Suddenly, I saw a ladder going up one column. I jumped onto it and started climbing as this behemoth demon closed the distance. I rose just in time to be out of its clutches. Soon after climbing my eyes began to adjust to the darkness. I could see the drop off and it looked like an abyss of blackness.

In the distance beyond the cliff, I could see another cliff and a stream of water running in a different direction. It flowed into another cave. I reached the ceiling and noticed huge statues at the top. These statues were shaped like hippopotamuses. The feet of these grotesque stone statues were fused to the ceiling. There were multiple figures in a straight line leading across the black abyss. I couldn't go back down. I could only go across.

Part II – Falling

I positioned my feet, rocked back and leaped as far I could. I landed on the hippo. After touching it, this rock creature suddenly sprang to life. It dawned on me that it was a gargoyle fixating its eyes on me as it shifted its body weight to one side. It snapped at me with all its strength. This zombie looking gargoyle wanted to eat me. By ducking to my left and holding onto its back legs, I forced it to miss me. It shifted its body back to take another snap at me. As it moved to spring at me, I made my move and jumped the next one.

I knew the next one would come alive as soon as I jumped on it, so while the first monster was winding up for its second bite, I used its body motion to my advantage. I was launched toward the other hippo-gargoyle and knew I had to keep the momentum. Eureka! I made it, landing on its stomach. The confidence in me kicked into overdrive, and I jumped to the third one keeping the momentum. I hit the third, but my foot slipped!

"Oh, no, I'm down!" I thought. My foot slipped causing me to lose my balance and fall backwards. Immense terror shook my body like a convulsion or being electrocuted. I fell into darkness. I noticed alligators in the water as I fell. The realization of knowing that I was plummeting to my death caused me to black out.

A Dream

I woke up in the fetal position wearing pajamas, sat up and looked over this room. The room was in a shape of a cube with another cube above that I thought I could climb into. As I moved to the next cube above me, I could imagine the situation from a third person perspective. I went into the third cubed room and saw a Japanese wearing a traditional green kimono woman preparing sushi. Passing by, I went into another room and saw the character, Mr. Miyagi from the movie *The Karate Kid* catching flies. I sat beside him and caught flies with him. I felt my body becoming very tight, and I started waking up.

I just woke up from this vision-dream and saw the doctors surrounding me. My body felt motionless as I tried to communicate with them. It was very hard, and I realized I was on tranquilizers. I knew it was a tranquilizer because during my high school years I experimented on lot of different things. I was able to yell at the doctors, "Stop giving me the ketamine or whatever you're giving me!" They looked at me dumbfound when I passed out again. It took every bit of energy to yell it out. I was in a sit-up like position and lost all strength after I yelled, falling backward onto pillow before blacking out.

Part III – Drowning

Asleep again, I picked up the vision where I left off, falling to my death in the first vision "Oh, my God!" I fell into an underground ocean and the water was roaring as waves crashed into each other. My eyes were still adjusting to the darkness, and I could see a massive battleship through the choppy water on the horizon. The ship had Nazi flags and signs on the stern. Massive holes were blown in the side of the ship, leading to the interior. There was no other place for me to go, so I swam towards the massive ship. With every stroke, I would gulp water and gasp for air.

Making it to the ship was a miracle. I managed to climb through the hole and could see a staircase one hundred feet away down the hallway. I made a run for it to get to the top. I ran as fast I could toward the staircase, pumping one leg in front of the other with long strides. Moving with a purpose, I reached the stairs and water started rushing in towards me. "Oh great, I'm going to drown," I thought. I had no other choice but to climb up as fast as I could. At the top of the first set, the stairs didn't go any higher. The ship was rocking back and forth, and water was flooding the halls. There was another staircase down toward the stern, and I ran for it.

Once there, I flew up the stairs like a fireman racing into a burning building. I got to the next deck, and the water was rushing up from the floor. Down the hall, the way was blocked by fire and rubble. I looked behind me and saw the only direction I could go. I ran as water was starting to rush in faster and faster. I ran into a room with no way out and looked back at the bulkhead. I ran to the door and struggled to close it against the rushing water. Closing the door was a struggle, but thankfully it was achieved. Adrenaline was surging through my body as if I were in a Hollywood action movie.

I shut the door and cranked down on the seal. I thought I could stop the water from rushing in, but now I was trapped. The water was still flowing in at a rapid speed through cracks all over. The thought of drowning and being isolated was overwhelming. Water was quickly shoulder height and then rose suddenly up to my head. Before I knew it, I was holding onto ceiling pipes. My head was now under water and I held my breath with everything I had. I knew it was a matter of time before I drowned, but my human instinct to survive was in overdrive. Fear overwhelmed me, I was mashing my eyes shut holding on to everything I had and suddenly I let go of the air in my lungs and choked in water before blacking out.

Part IV – Isolation

I woke up lying on a metal bed, constricted by a straitjacket. Lying downward at a forty-five-degree angle pushed more blood towards my head as I tried to look around. The room was an old surgical operating room with bricks outlining the walls and dome-shaped ceiling. There was moss on the walls and the smell of mildew filled the room. The only source of light was coming from the single light bulb eerily dangling from the ceiling. I could also see a glowing red and white exit sign at the end of a hallway. I was testing the strength of the straitjacket as my head swelled and the heat rose, becoming unbearable. Sweat was running down my face but also into my ears because of lying downward. I started screaming for help. I was screaming at the top of my lungs for someone to come to my aid. This place looked very old, and no one was there to help me. "Please, anyone, if you're out there, get me out of here!"

Hours went by, then days. I yelled and screamed, yelled more and screamed more. No one answered me. After feeling like weeks had gone by, my mind was losing control. I started blacking out but was fought it with all the energy I could muster. The burden was too much, and I lost conscience.

Another Dream

I found myself driving in a machete box-car on top of a water in Buffalo, New York with my Stepmother. Driving the car around the tower was pure excitement. We were driving in circles, kicking up dirt as we went. We both laughed at the excitement of zooming round and round, when suddenly the tower turned into a gumball machine. We were on the inside, driving around the glass bowl like a circus act dodging gumballs. I saw the exit at the dispenser and headed straight for it. The car went flying out of the gumball machine with us laughing and smiling.

I woke up looking across the room. I couldn't tell at first, but it looked like my brother Brian was with my Dad. I looked directly at my Father and told him I had to pee, I felt a huge rush to urinate. He assured me I was fine because I was hooked up to a super pubic catheter and shouldn't have to pee. I really had to go, so I pushed out everything in and then blacked out.

Part V – Torture

I woke up on the hospital bed and realized how badly I was injured. I could see my stumps where my legs once were. The room was covered in red lighting, and my bed was slowly turning to perpendicular to the room. I glanced down and saw the table with all the medical instruments and other barbaric looking surgical tools. I was strapped to the bed and saw a face mask on a table near the bed. The mask was strange with tubes in the mouth and nose area. As I looked around the room, there were giant metallic machines resembling a human-like war machine from the movie *Ironman*. Two doctors came into the room. The one closer to me was looking at the surgical tools. He didn't look at me, but said, "Don't worry, we're going to take good care of you. We will have you back in the war in no time. You actually get to pick one." He was referring to these man-sized machines. This reminded me of a futuristic movie setting where doctors would transfer the mind and soul from the body to the machine.

The technician looked at me, and I was stunned because his eyes were black. I couldn't see any pigment in his pure black eyes. Bewildered and confused, I struggled to free myself but the straps were too tight. Helpless, I couldn't move. I knew he was a demon.

"Don't worry," he said in a calming voice. "We have the technology now to put your mind right in there, and you can go back and fight as much as you want." The devilish man began grabbing the tools on the table and forcibly shoving tubes down my throat and nose. I struggled, but was weak while as he made his way with me. He attached sensors over my head and eyes. "Be very still now," he said calmly as his hand reached for the switch turning the machine on.

When machine was switched on it caused a vomiting sensation in me. It was different and more painful than anything I had endured. My whole body was catatonic and frozen. The force of this machine felt as if my spirit was violently pulled out of my body. Trying to hold onto my spirit was a sensation that cannot be explained, and just as I thought I lost my grip on my soul the technician switched the machine off. He was laughing, making little comments I couldn't quite understand, I was completely drained, gasping for air. He was speaking about wrongly calibrating the machine, and then he switched it on again and instantly the torture would hit me before he turned it off. He would turn it on again and suddenly turn it off. Shortly after, I realized I was being tormented by demons. They turned the system on higher and higher. This torturing process lasted for hours, to the point of physical and mental exhaustion.

I felt my spirit being ripped out of my blown-up body as I desperately grasped onto it with my teeth. I was sucked into this massive robot death machine. I could feel the circuitry rushing through me, robbing me of my voice. I could see through the metallic eyes, and soon realized I had no senses except the sight. I couldn't hear anything but the despair of my own thoughts. I couldn't feel anything because I lost the sense of touch. The entrapment and isolation was beyond claustrophobic. The devil looked straight into the machine's eyes. I could see them. They reached behind the head and switched me off.

Part VI – The Pit

I woke up being thrown into a deep hole. It was like a cistern. I could only see out of the top, everything else was black. I felt trapped inside unable to move like the character Newt captured by the Xenomorphs in the James Cameron film *Aliens*. I was stuck and alone. Soon I couldn't see anything but blackness. My mind grew exhausted as panic surged through my mind. Minutes turned into hours and hours turned to days. I screamed for help, and I called out a name I never used before: I called out to Jesus and then lost

conscience.

Heaven

A Final Dream

I saw my family pushing my hospital bed towards the movie theater. All of us were on our way to see the new *Captain America* film. As soon as we reached the door, the sky began to collapse and break into pieces, disappearing as it fell. The hospital hallway was on the other side of the door. I could see the Doctor and the nurses pushing me and running towards the elevator. We were going to surgery in a major hurry. I was still in my bed, and they held blood packets and IV bags in their hands, squeezing the fluids in me. Arriving in the elevator, they began chest compressions, and I saw my spirit rise out of my body.

Ascension

In a split second, my spirit shot up like a reverse lightning bolt going from the ground upward. I shot through the elevator shaft and ascended through the ceiling, penetrating the roof. As I looked down, I quickly saw the hospital shrink out of sight. I saw the face of the Earth, and it also shrank out of sight. Looking to my right, the stars looked like white streaks of light as I traveled faster and faster. I looked to the left and saw the same, and then I looked up. A large white light flashed in front of me like I was looking directly into the sun. The flash transitioned back to a clear view, and I saw I was in another world.

Just experiencing this sequence of events caused me to think about my situation immediately. I looked to my front, and saw three leaders in their battle uniforms speaking to each other. They were wearing highly advance battle armor. I looked down at my attire and saw the same uniform. Then I looked to my right and noticed I was at a combat outpost. Smoke from my peripheral vision caught my attention to the left. I looked there and saw massive destruction. Fire and black clouds billowed beyond the outpost, and I knew a massive war was taking place.

The sense of pure inspiration and urge to fight filled my body like an atomic adrenaline rush. I snapped my head forward and yelled, "Stop talking, let's go!" I was giving these orders as if I was the one in charge. Someone to the right glanced quickly, investigating who was shouting orders. He looked confused and immediately said, "Hey, you're not supposed to be here yet." Without thinking, I thrust my hand in the direction of the battle, shouting: "Forget all that, I'm here! Let's go!" The same one replied, "You made a bargain, don't you remember? You have to go back to Walter Reed, heal and fulfill your bargain." I paused, thought and then said, "Oh yeah." Suddenly, I noticed I was flying back towards Earth.

I could see China and Chinese jets flying through the cities. There were massive explosions, and liquid fire came raining from the sky. Nuclear bombs were fired and exploding in cities as fighter jets maneuvered around skyscrapers. Chinese flags were clearly visible as I was coming closer the ground. I could see the Chinese armies running through the cities slaughtering everything in sight, leaving no survivors. This was a massive nuclear war. My spirit was traveling through and inside the buildings. I noticed miraculously that I was back in a physical body trying to help and defend a certain skyscraper floor. Everything was on fire: the walls, the floor and the staircases. I was locked in a room, barricaded with another person, a woman. I could hear machine guns firing and explosions going off in the distance and then getting closer. The enemy breached the barricaded door sending debris everywhere. The Chinese forces stormed through the room and suddenly I was pulled from the battle, flying back towards America and finally to Walter Reed Military Hospital in Washington D.C.

While traveling back through the hospital and into my room, I watched my spirit enter back into my body. I felt weak as I woke up from that vision. Although I felt weak, the war was fresh in my mind. I looked to the right, saw my Dad sitting next to me, and said to him after my hellish visions: "Dad, nuclear war is no good." He looked back at me and said, "Tim, you were injured in Afghanistan. You're safe, and you're at Walter Reed." I quickly replied, "I know where I'm at!"

I experienced the most intense dreams and visions after nearly losing my life. I had seven visions, six of which were pure chaos and torment with no abatement in sight. Yet, the last was pure. The dreams and visions seemed so real that I could not erase them from my mind.

Walter Reed

Dad looked confused and told me how to use the pain medication. I started hitting the button, instantly feeling an enormous sense of relief. My dreams quickly disappeared from my mind as Dilaudid (hydromorphone) surged through my body. I thought, "This is awesome! Forget those dreams; I'm in the world."

I quickly started assessing my injuries and reached for my left leg. I noticed it was gone almost directly at my hip. I thought "okay," and felt the bandages covering my right leg. There were tubes attached to my leg and I quickly found out they were wound vacuums purging infectious tissue away from the wounds. I reached between my legs and was thankful, to say the least. I looked at my stomach with multiple staples going down my abdomen and to the left of my belly button I saw this plastic bag attached to me. There was fecal matter in the bag; it was a colostomy. I never even heard of this before, I was lucky to be alive at this point. I turned my attention and looked at my hands. I thought, "At least I could play video games still." I noticed metal bars coming out of my pelvis; it was an external fixator holding me together. I grabbed it confused, wondering what it was.

Later, doctors came in and told me my fight wasn't over. I was going into surgery a few times a day to clean my wounds and beat the infection. There was a flesh eating fungus making its way up my leg and they were removing portions of my leg to fight the infection. It was like going to the deli and getting a half-pound of ham. Zoom, zoom, off it comes and there goes more of my legs. The Doctors explained how I flat lined on them and nearly died. I had almost one hundred blood transfusions and more than a hundred medical procedures. My left arm had a team of fifteen doctors working tirelessly to save the skeletal aftermath. There were bandages over my arms and another external fixator going into my left thumb and hand.

The battle to save my legs began. The doctors told me the infections were spreading, and they needed to surgically remove my left hip. Being heavily medicated for weeks dulls the mind, but when they were talking about a hip disarticulation, I ask about the procedure. The next words shocked me. "We have to cut out your hip," the doctor said. I panicked. "No way are you taking my hip!" I shouted. I wasn't thinking about how severe the infection was, and my mom suggested praying. "Of course I will pray, whatever you want me to do," I desperately agreed, and we prayed to Jesus Christ to stop the infections. Later, one of the orthopedic surgeons came in to have a heart to heart talk with me. I didn't want to lose my hip; I already lost enough. The doctor explained that as soon as the infection gets into my abdomen, I would die. He asked me if I really wanted that, and shortly after that conversation I agreed to the surgery.

Mom was there in the room, and she was praying for me during the walk to surgery. She spoke with a senior orthopedic surgeon about saving my hip, questioning and interceding with doctors. I fell asleep knowing that I would wake up with my hip gone. I wondered how much more would I have to lose? Three hours later I woke up from surgery, and I was told the infections were slowing down and clearing up. So I was able to keep my hip.

Walter Reed was merging with the Bethesda Naval Hospital, and my surgery would be one of the last surgeries before the merger. The metal contraption that was holding my pelvis together was taken out three weeks early. By September, on the eve of nine eleven, I was notified I was transitioning from an inpatient to outpatient status. I began physical therapy; it was strenuous after such trauma and lying in bed for weeks.

Before being wounded, I weighed 245 pounds and was bench-pressing nearly four hundred pounds. Now, weeks after the injury, my arms were the size of toothpicks. The explosion took everything I had, but my body held onto life. I started showing improvement even though I weighed less than 150 pounds.

I had multiple teams of doctors from all the specialty departments in the hospital. I was prescribed a multitude of medications, although I wondered why I was on so many, I took them as directed. Antibiotics were fed into me intravenously nonstop to fight infections. I was told I would be discharged from the hospital on October 20 to start the next phase of my recovery. The doctors tallied up my surgeries, and I had endured around one hundred twenty by that time. I had a long way to go one urologist told me; he also said if I really wanted to heal quickly I would also need to heal the mind, body, and the spirit.

Upon being discharged, mom and I had a falling out between the two of us, and it stemmed from the conflict between her and father. The animosity between the both of them was rooted in their divorce nearly twenty-five years before my accident. The doctors were preparing my discharge and asked me who I wanted to be my non-medical attendee. Due to the circumstances, I chose my Dad because we're both men, and I felt more comfortable. My Mom left the hospital abruptly because of the tension from our falling out. Dad was my non-medical attendee, and he had to help me with all follow-up doctor appointments.

I was given an electric wheelchair from Mr. Lancaster of American Mobility. This chair was beastly. It could go anywhere and was controlled by a little joystick on the right side. As weak as I was, I couldn't do much. But having independence was extremely uplifting. I wasn't trapped in the hospital any more. I had the freedom to go where I pleased.

It was two weeks before discharge, and I was taken off all intravenous medication and was only taking pills. There was an announcement on our floor, and we were told to stay in the hospital room. Rumors circulated that President Obama was coming to visit us, and a few hours later he made his appearance in my room, thanking me for my service to the United States of America as he handed me his Presidential coin. I humbly accepted the coin, and then he shook hands with my Dad. After leaving, I rolled out to the parking garage and spent some time smoking cigarettes with my dad. We were amazed about the visit and being so close to the President. The next week we were invited to the White House for a tour and during the visit, President Obama made a guest appearance to all of us. He walked right up to me, looked me in the eyes, then pointing at me saying, "I know you!" I had a huge smile on my face and was astonished he remembered. Being at the hospital, there are multiple opportunities for tours and visits, and I wanted out of the environment altogether, so all this was well received by me.

Building 62 was our living quarters after being discharged as an inpatient. I was being assigned to this brand new building designed specifically for catastrophically injured soldiers. There was an army of us soldiers during the summer of 2011, and the building was filling up very quickly. The Bethesda Naval Hospital is large like a small town. Our living quarters were located directly across the hospital in front of physical therapy center known as MATC (Military Advance Training Center).

The room was a two-bedroom apartment equipped with everything that we would need. There was a massive dinning facility on the first floor, and the Warrior Transition Brigade was located between the two apartment wings. I was assigned a nurse case manager who oversaw my care plan. He was very professional and cared very much about my needs through the healing process.

I had a laundry list of medications I was prescribed, and I needed to take some on an hourly basis. I was having blood work done every few weeks because of the blood I received overseas. There was such a shortage of blood that calls would go over the base in Afghanistan calling for all soldiers who were A-negative to run to the trauma center. Their blood would go out of them and directly into me. It was as if the blood was coming out as they were putting it in. It took roughly ten grown men to save my life.

I went to physical therapy at MATC every day, and my physical therapist, Bob, was one of the nicest men that I had met. He was preparing me for prosthetic work, the plan was to get fitted for prosthetics and learn to walk again. I also had two follow-up surgeries that forced me to delay physical therapy; it was like taking a step forward and then two back.

Halloween

On Halloween, I had the worst weekend of my life. That weekend a lot of people were visiting us. My girlfriend was there, my brother Andrew, his wife, and my stepmother. We were out that evening at the restaurant Dave and Busters, hosted by the Aleethia Foundation. This foundation would host a dinner every Friday night to get us off the naval base. On this particular evening, I felt an urge I haven't felt in months. It felt like I had to go to the bathroom. I shouldn't have felt that urge because I was using a colostomy bag. It didn't feel right, and my stomach hurt. I felt the urge to leave dinner. After leaving and getting back to the building on base, I just laid in bed all night tossing and turning. I could not fall asleep. If I lay on my back it hurt, and if I lay on my stomach, it hurt more. I was very uncomfortable.

In the morning, I made the decision to go to the emergency room to be evaluated. I waited four hours to be seen. The doctor looked very familiar, and it turned out he was one of the surgeons that worked on my leg. He was an average sized man with small hands and he performed his exam on me. It was very uncomfortable, especially finishing with a rectal exam. I was in an incredible amount of pain. He concluded that I had fecal matter lodged in my lower bowel, and it has been stuck up there for the past four months. He prescribed a home enema and suppositories with the hope I could dislodge the fecal matter. I took the prescription and went back to my room.

As soon as I returned there, the pressure in my abdomen was beginning to hurt badly. I went into the bathroom and worked up the courage to self-administer a suppository the size of my pinky. The capsule ruptured almost immediately, and I could feel a greasy substance inside of me. It wanted out quick, and there's nothing holding it back. I leaped onto the toilet with adrenaline. I felt so much pressure it brought me to tears, the huge mass inside was like a rock and it wanted out. The mass was not coming out, and I began to bleed. There was so much pressure I couldn't hold it. I thought I pushed something out, but when I looked down there was nothing but blood. The grease was still inside, and the pressure was continuing to build. Straining for two hours left me completely exhausted, and I was embarrassed to face this situation. I was so exhausted I couldn't get off the toilet. I called for my younger brother to come in and help me. I didn't want my dad or girlfriend to help; I needed my brother.

He came into the bathroom, and I was crying from all the pain. As a result, he started crying as well. I told him to stop it because he was supposed to be the strong one. He picked me up and put me back in my chair. The whole ordeal lasted for hours, and I found myself going back to the emergency room. The first doctor I saw had already left. The new doctor that saw me looked like Shrek. I could not believe how tall this man was; he looked like an ogre. He appeared to be seven feet tall, and his hands were immense, "Oh my God!" I demanded to see another doctor but couldn't because of the shift change. I asked, "Is there anyone else I can see?" There wasn't.

I briefed Dr. Shrek on what I thought my problem was when he interrupted me and said: "let me do my job." I told him I didn't want his sausage fingers inside of me, so he then ordered an x-ray. After the x-ray, the doctor came back in the room and told me I am lucky to be alive. I should have gone septic after a few weeks. The massive feces resembled the size of dinosaur eggs, and with a concerned look and demeanor, the doctor said he was getting it all out right now. The danger was so high he went to work right away.

I told the Doctor, "Hey can I have some valium or something strong?" I knew that this was about to be a horrendous experience, and I was already on a bunch of medications. I was on Oxycodone instant release, Oxycodone sustained-release, methadone, gabapentin, different nerve blocks, anti-depressants, anti-psychotics, blood thinners and a laundry list of anti-inflammatories and stool softeners. The pain medications weren't helping that much, and I knew this would be horrible. The doctor told me I was on the way to many medicines as is, and without further warning he started roto-rooting my lower bowel. I could feel tremendous pressure as my Dad accompanied me through this ordeal. I was yelling out in pain with nothing to compare it to. I hadn't gone to the bathroom in over three months.

I screamed in pain, demanding some sort of medication and yelling for valium. I knew it would knock me out. The doctor still wouldn't give it to me. I cried for hours, and hugged onto my Dad as the doctor and nurses propped me up on my side. I held onto my Dad as hard as I could, I must have left bruises on him from how hard I was squeezing. This was pure hell that I was enduring. I was thinking about so many different things in addition to the pain. No one deserves this suffering; it was too much to endure. I thought about the men that had blown me up and now were dead. I thought if they were in hell, I would forgive them and bring them back to ease my suffering. I passed out from all the pain and anguish.

I woke up around seven o'clock in the morning feeling a dripping sensation from my lower bowel. It felt as if some of the pressure was gone, and I asked the nurses if they had gotten it all out. They told me that after two enemas, soap suds and suppositories, they hadn't gotten anything out. The doctor also said, "Hey, no problem we'll discharge you, and you can come back Monday to see a specialist." With all the pain I endured and no resolution, I told the doctor there was no way I would leave and to admit me now.

I was admitted right then, and by noon a specialist was called in to deal with this situation. The technician came over to me, and I realized it was another doctor who I already knew. He was a general surgeon, and he assured me I was going to be fine. He said he was sorry about all that I had to endure. The operating room was prepared, and I went in for surgery. After surgery, the doctor came back to me and said "Listen, this is critical. I'm going to have you stay until Monday and as soon as you get upstairs, tell the tending nurse to get you your medications. Your meds will wear off soon, and your pain will be coming back by then."

I didn't feel any pain and the pressure was gone. I felt lighter and great. I was taken to the monitoring floor where I previously was during my inpatient stay. As soon as I got to the floor, I told the Asian nurse who spoke very bad English to have my medications ready. She left the room and about forty-five minutes later I started to feel a great sense of pain, it was growing stronger, quickly. The nurse came back in the room, asking me if I needed anything, and I told her loudly to get my medications. She looked confused because she didn't know what my medications were, so I told her as I squirmed in bed to look at my chart or on the computer. The pain was becoming more and more unbearable, so I told her to go quickly. The nurse came in the third time and said: "Mr. Payne, where is your pain?" I looked at her and felt as if all time stopped and shouted: "in my asshole!" She left my room, and my girlfriend was now there instead of my Dad. I asked her to hand me my bag, and I pulled out my Oxycodone and ate five of them. I went to sleep. Shortly after, I woke up hours later to the nurse trying to determine what medications I still needed.

The next day the general surgeon team came in and suggested I have a colostomy reversal since my lower bowel was working regularly. It was the sign they needed. Having a colostomy was tough psychologically, and I wanted to have the reversal as soon as I could. My Dad had to change my bag for me because my left hand wasn't very functional. I tried to deal with everything from day to day. Yet, after this horrific ordeal, I began to dislike Halloween, thinking the devil was trying to kill me.

Physical Recovery

The colostomy reversal was scheduled by the end of 2011, and it went smooth even though I had more follow-up surgeries to get through. The next month in January, I had my ear drum replaced to celebrate the New Year. As time went on, the residual femurs started showing signs of heterotopic ossification, which meant that the bone was growing abnormally. Horned shaped spurs were forming at the tips of the amputation sites and trying to walk would cause more problems.

Before the end of January, I was shocked to find out my Dad was leaving me. He said he couldn't afford to stay with me anymore and he had to go back to work. I was distraught with what was happening, but understood where he was coming from. With all other options exhausted, I asked my girlfriend who just graduated college to come help and she agreed. After she had moved from Buffalo to Bethesda, everything was moving at a constant rate and more changes were on the horizon.

Next, my nurse case manager would be replaced with another nurse. The second nurse case manager wasn't as cool as the first. I met her with my girlfriend in her office on the third floor of Building 62. As soon as I rolled into her office, I noticed between thirty and forty little rubber ducks on her desk. The ducks were dressed like different characters, Halloween, sports teams, emergency service personnel, soldiers and a laundry list of other characters. I thought it was a grand display of rubber ducks and without thinking, I said: "Someone likes rubber ducks."

That turned out to be a wrong thing to say, and the look on her face turned wicked. She snarled at me, snapped he chin up and said, "My patients gave me those." I thought this is how the relationship would be. "Ma'am, I didn't mean anything by that," I said to her. She went over my medical plan, ignoring my comment, asking me multiple questions. I was then told to contact her every Wednesday to review my appointments. I explained to her that I was scheduled to receive an adaptive van, and was planning to walk after my heterotopic ossification surgery.

By March, I had the surgery and received the van from an organization called Help Our Military Heroes. The van was a major blessing from the non-profit organization based out of Danbury, Connecticut. However, the surgery was extremely painful. Before the operation, I decided not to get the nerve block below my waist. I didn't want the nerve block because I disliked having q catheter. The doctors explained how they were going to cut down to the bone, separate the muscle from bone, and saw out the abnormal bone growth. After the bone was removed, the remaining bone would have to be prepared for myodesis. This refers to the anchoring of residual muscle or tendon to residual bone using sutures that are passed through small holes at the anchoring point.

After the surgery and before opening my eyes, I woke up screaming. I could feel a great sense of pain; the doctors asked me to assess my pain on a scale from one to ten with ten being the worst. Well, the pain I had was way over ten. It felt like someone dropped a thousand pounds on my legs. I was screaming for the nerve block immediately, and on the spot, the nurses and doctors quickly went into action and put me at ease. Within minutes of enduring this unbearable pain, they were able to help.

I planned to stay in the hospital bed for two weeks but managed to leave after five days. They cut me all the way to the bone, and my legs were as swollen as basketballs. I stayed in the room until the nerve block was taken out, and then I could get rid of the catheter I hated. The sutures were massive, surrounding my nubs. And after two weeks the swelling went down, the incisions closed and the sutures were removed. My girlfriend was so patient with me that I wanted to do something nice, so we planned a trip to Disney world a month later.

We left for Disney in April. I was trying to wean myself off the medications and decided to leave them at the hospital. On the way to Florida, we stopped in Charleston, South Carolina to visit my friend Jeremy. While staying at the hotel, I was lying in the bed and rolled to my side. As soon as I turned onto my side, I felt a mass pull off the tip of my right residual leg. Pain shot through my leg. I knew something was wrong. It felt like the muscle dislodged itself from the suture holes in the bone. I froze and couldn't move at all from the pain; I lay in the bed motionless for the remainder of the night.

I dealt with this pain from the failed myodesis. We continued our vacation and soon after arrived at the place where dreams come true. My girlfriend's smile made the trip there worth it. I managed to make it through the week, and after arriving back, I was back on the pain medications. It was so painful being at Disney.

After eight weeks post-surgery, the pain from my legs never went away. I was also doing the best I could to walk on prosthetics. It was extremely difficult in my case due to how short my limbs were. I had seven inches of bone on my right leg and about an inch and a half on the left. Getting prosthetics that could fit seemed to always be the challenge. I could only walk a few laps at a time due to fitting and pain. After a few laps on the track they would fall off. Wearing liners as a barrier between the skin and the device would cause slippage because of the lack of bone.

I would try to walk daily; in the meantime, I also saw my nurse case manager. She was happy to hear about the surgery and the trip to Disney. She asked me how I liked traveling from   place to place was now that I had a van. I told her was giving me some independence. After our conversation, she started explaining to me how I didn't need a nonmedical attendee, and I was fully capable of taking care of myself. My demeanor changed instantly, one I had thought she was attentive to my care and now she appeared to be stripping me of my non-medical attendee Just four months after my girlfriend arrived, I now had to fight to keep her here with me.

I told my manager that I couldn't do everything on my own, I was still adjusting and would need more surgeries. How was I supposed to take out the trash with a cast on my arm and no legs? She never offered any solution but rather a deadline for her departure. I left her office and went back to my room to speak with my girlfriend. I realized at this point I had to be very careful with what I said and to whom I say it. After a long conversation and trying to determine the best course of action, my girlfriend and I decided to get married. Right after I woke up from a two week of coma after the accident, I didn't want to see my girlfriend. I wanted to break up with her. I thought how could anyone want to be with a freak? She told me that she loved me and would be there for me. I felt as if we were making the best decision. Now, if she was my spouse, they couldn't make her leave. We decided to get married mid-June and during this process, my manager was creating more problems by having us removed from Building 62.

I complained and tried to switch case managers but it wasn't working. Every month, the Army would have us injured soldiers complete a self-assessment online based on our care. I was completely honest, and I wouldn't have been able to do this if it weren't for my social worker. I was honest with the social worker about all the opposition I was facing.

He looked me in the eyes and told me I had to fight with the pen and keep on going. He told me not to give up and to fill out those assessments because at the top, the commanders read them.

I unleashed a firestorm testimony every month detailing the mental anguish interfering with my recovery. I wasn't making progress; my nurse case manager did not relent from her position to have us removed from the building. The person who read my reports must not have been at the top of the command chain because I knew the General took his job very seriously.

My newlywed and I moved off the base right after we were married and moved to downtown Silver Spring, right outside Bethesda. We settled in and continued with my medical plan. I was continuing to fill out the self-assessments monthly, and my follow up surgeries would continue. I had a tendon transfer on my left hand later in September. By this time, I already reached my "alive day," July 3, so it had now been a year after my injuries. I didn't think much of it due to the constant pace and current circumstances. I was heavily prescribed different types of medications, and over the year I felt numb to the world. I was just going with the flow at this point, I felt the pain would never end.

When the doctors started adding nerve medications to my regimen, I blew up like a balloon. Over the course of the year, I managed to gain all my weight back. Before I was injured, I weighed two hundred forty five pounds with my legs, and at that point I weighed the same without them. One of my best friends saw how big I was getting, and he gave me a quick call. It was nice hearing Jeremy again, and I will never forget what he said to me: "Tim, hey man I saw you're walking that's awesome! But dude, you're looking pretty fat man, what happened? I thought you're a special soldier." His words penetrated through my numbness, causing me to think.

I knew that I had to do something, but I didn't know what to do. It got me thinking more.

Veterans Day was closely approaching as we continued the same routine and my wife's annual trip to Florida was coming up. She would always travel with her mother and two brothers. I was invited to come, but I had no interest in going to the beach based on how I looked. I didn't want people staring at me, and I didn't want to get stuck in sand, so I stayed at home. One of my friends from High School invited me down to his place in North Carolina. The holiday weekend was rapidly approaching, and I submitted a pass to travel out of the area. It was my first time going anywhere alone. I always had someone with me, but this time, I didn't.

Seeing my battle buddy was a blessing. He told me that I should get off the medications and just smoke some dope instead. I thought to myself, at this point in my life I don't even care. So, I took the pipe with marijuana when suddenly out of nowhere, I felt the same presence as I had in Afghanistan come back to me like a rushing wind. I heard a voice say, "Get off all the medications right now! It's killing you!" I felt consciousness rise through the numbness. It was as if I could see an overhead view of the entire year and how the medication was affecting me. I previously thought if I didn't have the drugs, I would experience physical pain. I was so dependent on the medication, I couldn't see how it was slowly killing me.

After the long weekend, I made my way back to the hospital and made an appointment with my primary care doctor. I also learned that my nurse case manager was no longer working for the warrior transition brigade. I was being reassigned to a new manager. I met with my primary care doctor and explained to her what I did over the long weekend. I realized how the medications were robbing me of my own mind, and now I wanted to fight back. I told her I was getting off the drugs, and she insisted I stay on them. I told her I didn't want them anymore, but she insisted again that I stay on the plan. I yelled at her, and told her it's my body and it's my plan.

I thought about detox and what I learned during my recruiting job. Physical fitness pushes drugs out of the system. I also was thinking about eating healthier to cleanse my body as well. I turned my thoughts into action, but due to the damage of my left arm, I couldn't lift weights and working out would be limited. I thought swimming would be the next best thing. I devised a plan to start eating healthy and swimming regularly after the New Year.

I quit taking my medication – nearly twenty different types – and started experiencing the effects of withdrawal. I had hot and cold sweats, became more irritable and was dry heaving uncontrollably. I decided to continue taking methadone and slowly wean myself off of it. I cut the pill in half, then a week later cut the halves in half and then a week later continued the cycle until I was taking a small fraction of the pill. Finally I was off the medication by January and by February I had quit smoking cigarettes as well.

The physical recovery took over a year and follow up surgeries also meant taking steps backward from the progress I was making. I didn't realize how obese I had become because of the amount of medication the doctors were prescribing to me. I had to take matters into my own hands and became my own healthcare advocate.

Suicide

When I first went to the pool, I told myself, "I have to start somewhere." I remember looking in the mirror at how big I had become. I looked like a walrus, but I had to do the best I could and set new habits that were good for me. I motivated myself to try and as soon as I arrived at the pool, I imagined I looked like big fat walrus rolling off the wheelchair and plunking into the pool. I waved my arms in a freestyle motion and slowly gained momentum. I managed to finish only five laps because I was so weak. I was dead tired. But, this was my starting point and soon after I realized how boring swimming can be.

During the first week, I could only swim about five laps at a time. I was changing the way I ate and made healthier choices. In a few short weeks, I found myself able to swim ten laps and then fifteen. While swimming, it's only you and the water and you're trapped in your own mind. The throbbing pain in my legs wasn't getting any better, but swimming gave me a way to channel the pain. I discovered how fitness came and alleviate pain.

Soon I could swim forty laps, and that's when I began dwelling on the past. I was thinking about all my failures and how I never achieved my goals. I sustained injures during Ranger training, re-directed orders when I tried Special Forces, another injury during the qualifying course and finally receiving assignment orders for Fort Drum after being selected for civil affairs. To make matters worse, I was accepted to civil affairs and received a class date after I had been blown up. Why did I make it through all this? Why am I alive? This all sucks. I started feeling more and more like a failure and now everything seemed out of reach.

I had tried my best to live by the Army Values, and I was becoming more and more depressed about my injuries, feeling like I had nothing else to live for. I had interests in bioengineering and regenerative medicine, but I was getting tired of fighting. I started thinking there was no point to all this. Soon after, my thoughts turned to anger. While swimming, I was exerting myself as hard as possible and yelling at myself, calling myself a failure. I started yelling at a God that I didn't know existed.

I began yelling at God while swimming, saying, "Why am I still alive? Just kill me. I don't know this Jesus guy, but I know you killed him because of sin. Why don't you just kill me the same way and make me something useful!" I didn't want to fight anymore, and as a result, I started devising a plan to end my suffering.

I thought about my soldiers. I didn't want to fail them. I didn't want them to know what I was about to do. Sadly, I starting thinking about ways to kill myself without them finding out. I thought I could make it seem like an accident. My plan was to force myself into a heart attack. I heard of heart failure during physical training, and I thought if I could get stimulants as a medication, I could take them and over-exercise. I knew it was the only way to end my suffering, so I manipulated my neurologist into prescribing stimulants.

I was swimming forty laps at a time, and soon I was able to swim seventy-five laps and then one hundred. I was incredibly focused on accomplishing my suicide goal, and I could feel my heart pounding as a result. It felt like a freight train was moving inside of me as my heart pounded harder and harder.

I was attending physical therapy, though without any progress because of my prosthetics, which didn't fit right. I eventually gave up on the idea of walking. While in treatment, I saw a hand cycle on the floor and thought I could pick up handcycling as well. I went to the hand cycle clinic to meet the head coach of Ride-2-Recovery, a non-profit organization that promotes healing through bike riding with team working together. I was fitted for a cycle and told to ride only seven miles that first time. I was giving it everything I had and the seven miles was pretty easy. The coach asked me if I wanted to go for a ride the next day in Reston, Virginia even though it was fifty-miles long. I accepted immediately and thought of it as an opportunity to force my heart to explode.

I was riding regularly and swimming as much as I could. By April, almost two years after my accident, my wife and I began planning a bigger wedding to celebrate our union with family and friends. I kept my innermost feelings from her by wearing the fake mask that everything was awesome.

My new plan was very simple. I would take all my pre-workout supplements and then swim for two hours, covering approximately two miles, and then directly after climb onto the bike and ride for another two hours, about twenty-five miles. I covered almost 200 miles in May of 2013. There were times that I pushed so hard, I could literally feel my heart pounding through my chest and thought any second it was about to explode. It motivated me even more, but then suddenly would it stop. I pushed myself harder and harder over the threshold. I would think, here comes the heart attack, here it comes, then nothing. "I can't even kill myself?" I thought.

After a few months of riding with Ride-2-Recovery, I became encouraged by the participation of different riders.

There was an army of us injured soldiers. Being with a group and traveling together turned out being very enjoyable. We talked about war stories and the adversities we faced. Not long after, I went to my first bike marathon in Chicago. By the time summer ended, I had lost almost forty pounds and felt great because of all the physical exercise. I didn't even realize how my body adapted to the physical pain that I endured months before. I blew pass my second anniversary from the injury and just kept on swimming.

My mind adapted to the physical pain due because of my workout routine. I was working-out and spending time with my wife. I finally started enjoying life again without realizing what I had gone through. I quit smoking cigarettes and all medication earlier that year, and my mental resilience flourished. I didn't realize the battle I nearly lost as feverishly tried to self-induce cardiac arrest.

Chicago

I went to Chicago with the Achilles Freedom team out of New York City. The founder, Dick Traum, was the first amputee to run a marathon and his non-profit organization continues to help other ill or injured people participate in such events. On this trip to Chicago, the host of Achilles Freedom Team, Janet Patton, gave all our members the red carpet treatment when we traveled throughout the city. Her quirky, bubbly personality and cute joking was a blessing to all those who have the pleasure of meeting her.

The flight to the city was sponsored by the Veterans Airlift Command, a non-profit that helps injured veterans travel to and from certain locations by donating the use of private jets owned by corporate CEO's from various industries. The whole experience motivated me to keep pushing and think positive. On the flight to the city, the shared owners of this jet accompanied me, and that's when I met Stephanie Cooper, who is one of the coordinators of this organization. Getting to know her and her husband and hearing why they put the organization together was very heart warming. I could see how so many people put forth a lot of effort to help soldiers like myself adjust to our new way of life.

The Freedom team consisted of wounded veterans, but the organization also invited different chapters come from all over the world. This was a group of many people with some traveling from as far as South Africa. During the stay, I met a fellow veteran amputee who is from Detroit. When Nick and I first started talking, he was worried about his home and how deficit spending was collapsing their city. He voiced his concerns about economic collapse and civil unrest. I had no idea what he meant or what he was talking about, so I let him finish his story without comment, but it stuck with me. I was thinking about what he said, especially his ideas about civil unrest. The marathon was over before we knew it. The trip to Chicago and racing through its streets motivated more. I began to feel a sense of purpose. I began to think positive for the first time in years with the aid of cheering spectators who seemed to support us. After the marathon we all loaded back up on private jets and made our journeys back to our homes.

Plans Change

As soon as I arrived back to Bethesda, I was notified that my retirement was being pushed through the bureaucracy, and I would be leaving in a few short months. With retirement a reality, I began to think about what Nick said in Chicago. While driving back and forth to the hospital, I could see numerous Vietnam veterans' homeless and begging for money on the sides of the street. I thought about how they ended up in their predicament and that I didn't want to share their fate and fail to provide for myself or my family.

After being injured, I had to adapt completely to a new way of life. I was extremely interested in regenerative medicine and the cutting edge technology with the use of stem cells. I spent a lot of time at the hospital reading articles about emerging physical regeneration technologies. While reading, I thought about the comic book villain "The Lizard" in the Spider-man series and his penchant to use his own research for his self-gain. This character was also an amputee, and he recklessly used his technology to heal himself. As a result, he became a monstrous lizard terrorizing New York City. My transitioning goals would include this type of work, and I came up with a plan very quickly. I was reading and studying up on these things throughout my stay at Walter Reed Bethesda Naval Hospital. The best university I could attend was Wake Forrest in Winston-Salem, North Carolina.

Once I formulated a plan for school, I was still thinking about what Nick said in Chicago. I thought I should know how the economy works since I would be transitioning from the Army to an entirely different life. I retired after eleven years in the Army and now would be a citizen no longer fighting for freedom.

I started reading articles and reports about the economy by well-known economists such as Jim Rickards, Gerald Celente, Peter Schiff, Max Kaiser and Mike Maloney. I could see that the architecture of deficit spending leads to a crumbling economy and then the end result would be financial collapse. I saved all my pay before being injured and had multiple stocks in various companies revolving involved in stem cell research and new technologies like three-dimensional printing. I could see the cycle of collapse and how trillions of dollars in debt could never be paid off. I became afraid of how the country continued to spend its way to collapse. I made a rational decision to divert all my assets out of stocks to just break even. I transitioned my IRA into precious metals. The logic behind my decision stemmed from the simple fact that gold and silver cannot be printed like Federal Reserve notes. I was choosing sound money over fiat currency. Sound money is metal chiming, confirming the authenticity and value of the monetary asset. Fiat currency is ink on paper, declared valuable from a government-based trust. What happens when that government isn't working for the people?

During my independent research, I stumbled on a series known as "Hidden Secrets of Money" found at www.hiddensecretsofmoney.com. There are now six episodes, which describe the history of money and where it all began. The show also surveys the cycle of empires and how they rise and collapse throughout ancient and modern civilizations. Those cycles do not disappear, and as Winston Churchill once said: "The farther you look into the past, the farther you can see into the future." Churchill was speaking of the cycles and how the world truly works.

I was really intrigued by the history of what had transpired and grew more interested to learn more. I told my wife what I was doing, and by December, only a month after riding in Chicago, I asked her to participate in learning the history. She was too busy with her own interests, but I told her that I would pull out of the stock market and transition my assets to precious metals. I asked her to learn the same financial principles should something happen to me. I didn't want her to be unprepared if I unexpectedly died; I thought we could learn together.

With this as a backdrop, I continued to train daily for different marathons. As I was swimming, I would always think about staying motivated and living by the Army values, the Soldiers Creed and the Creed of Noncommissioned Officers. Verses from the creed, such as being proud of the Corps of Noncommissioned officers and bringing credit upon the Corp regardless of the situation I found myself in, really resonated with me.

The Army informed us that our separation date would be February 7, and I felt bad about not being able to help my wife pack our apartment during the transition. I knew her brother Stephen was available and suggested she ask him for help. I would be unable to do much, though I wanted to contribute in some way. I offered to pay her brother five hundred dollars in addition to his travel expenses like food and gas to come help us pack. I also thought we could spend time together visiting the sites at the national mall. It seemed like a "win, win situation" for all of us. I could now alleviate some of the stressors from moving. I made it a point for her to tell him to be with us on February 5. It was the best timing since we were leaving that weekend.

After Christmas and the beginning of New Year, we traveled to North Carolina and found a place to live. It was close to the private school for regenerative medicine, and we agreed on an apartment to keep costs low. We went to a furniture store to furnish our new home and traveled back home to Buffalo, New York afterward. We were able to share the news with our family, and then we headed back to Washington D.C.

I forgot to ask her if she told Stephen to come help, and when I mentioned it, she said she didn't ask him. I had been gone most of the day since the Army had me attending a lot of classes to prepare myself for the transition. These were long days with arriving home in the late evening. When I came home, I found myself asking her same two questions, "Did you look into precious metals? And did you ask your brother for help?" She said that she forgot or didn't do it yet. Days and weeks went by with this same routine, but I wanted my wife to be happy and decided to let it go.

After a week, I became increasingly upset because she wasn't doing anything during our transition from the military. She wasn't working. She would be at home while I was at the hospital all day. I would question myself about her behavior, and there were times she would tell me to leave her alone. After another week of this, I considered calling her brother myself but I didn't want to overstep my bounds. I wanted to see if she would work with me on this.

We argued a lot. I would try and stay motivated by continuing to work out and stay abreast of current events. After some arguments, she would just cry while I asked simple questions. I didn't understand the problem was. I started to think she didn't want to be a part of my future. I thought this because every time we would go home, she would cry and express frustration about leaving the D.C. area. I felt bad, and we weren't talking. She never asked her brother to come help us move.

On February 5, I had everything just about ready to be moved. Our apartment was partially packed up, and I made a Ride-Away appointment for the conversion van. I inadvertently missed the appointment because I was watching a YouTube documentary about people dying and going missing in National State Parks. This was around one o'clock in the afternoon. Five hours later, my wife received a phone call from her mother, and I heard her shout very frantically. I could see her trembling and her eyes began to tear up. I thought instantly something bad had happened. She looked at me and said her brother was dead. He fell off a cliff while walking in a state park.

Stephen (Acts 7)

Stephen was twenty-one when he fell into the gorge at Letchworth State Park. An avid and experienced outdoorsman, he was hiking alone. He was very physically fit and the most positive person I think I've met. I would consider him to be the rock of their family. He was a strong persona with a very loving personality. Always in the holiday spirit, he would decorate his room. He and I were always talking about movies, healthy living, traveling and fitness. He was a real brother to me, and when I first met him we connected instantly. He slipped off of a cliff during a terrible winter storm; but because of his strength, he initially survived the two-hundred-foot fall. He was able to call 9-1-1 numerous times, and gave emergency personnel his location. The service wasn't the best in the area, but the emergency personnel were able to triangulate his location with his cell phone. The phone calls were coming in and then suddenly stopped. He passed away from his injuries and exposure from the elements before medical help could arrive. After his passing, everything I went through came back like a tidal wave.

Survivors Guilt

After my wife received the horrifying news, I provided the best support I could. I told her not to blame herself or think if he had helped us move, he would be alive. I explained to her that we couldn't change what had happened. We cried over the loss.

We had to leave Walter Reed as quickly as possible. I called the command and told them about our loss. I finished clearing the unit the next day. The cadre came to our apartment and packed everything in a less than a few hour hours. They also packed our U-Haul and were extremely helpful. We were cleared from the Army, and our plan was to drop everything off at the apartment in North Carolina and drive straight home to Buffalo afterward.

We drove to Winston-Salem on Friday, February 7, and thankfully Matthew Canup, one of my best friends from the 82nd Airborne Davison, who lived in the same town, offered to help us unpack. We spent the night in our new apartment and left early in the morning to make our way home. On the way, I had time to begin thinking about of all the things that had transpired. It was like a tidal wave hitting me instantly. I was angry on the inside, and thought why did he died and not me. If anyone should be dead, it should be me. I felt guilty about my own survival. If I could, I would have traded places with him.

Reflection

Sergeant Alvin York became a Medal of Honor recipient during World War One. He was a big time troublemaker until he found faith in Jesus Christ. He was struck by lightning and it straightened him out. After World War I broke out, he became of conscientious objector but was drafted into the army. He objected to fighting, although later agreed and he became a highly decorated soldier. The man is a true American Hero.

I began to reflect about everything that happened to me and realized I fought through suicide and medication addiction. I saw things right after injury during my two weeks in hell/medicated coma. I made two prayers that actually came true. I started thinking that this was a sign, and I felt compelled to trace my steps backward.

I had some major events take place in my life: one was graduating from High School and the other, retiring from the Army. These were major life changing events, which caused me to shift gears emotionally. I was planning to attend college for film production after High School, but then 9/11 happened a month after graduating High School. And I joined the Army instead. Something similar happened after my wife's brother had passed away. That event changed my life and set me on a different course. I had to figure out what this may have meant, if anything.

I thought about the similarities between the two transition points in my life. I started thinking more about everything, and how I had been through so many trials. The visions I had after my injury were beginning to resonate with me unlike they had before. I thought more and more about what it meant to be alive. I knew I had to figure out the meaning of life and became focused on the life after death.

My Mom and I reconciled before Stephens's funeral, realizing that life is short and she had the right to know what happened. She attended the funeral service with us. After spending a lot of time home, my wife and I returned to North Carolina. I told my wife my concerns about our relationship and was honest about my suicide battles, addiction to medication and marijuana use. She told me that I was a drug addict and argued with me. Struggling to voice my concerns, I managed to share what I remembered about my visions while I was medically induced coma and the two prayers I made before the attack that injured me. I asked her if she would help me because I was confused. She refused to help, and I was sympathetic to this because she had just lost her brother.

The Harbinger

I looked into new age religion, thinking that in today's world it would be easier to find answers since scientist have probably figured it all out. On my quest for truth, I considered different concepts about our spirits and read about different religions. I looked into prayer but nothing seemed to answer my questions satisfactorily.

I called my Mom and told her briefly about my concerns, and she gave me a book called *The Harbinger* by Jonathan Cahn. I told her I wanted answers and not a book, so I was kind of upset. I didn't want to read anything to be honest, but after reading the back cover, I soon realized it could be helpful. It was about a warning to a nation on 9/11, the economic collapse of 2008 and what was on the horizon. What is more, it correlated those events with the fall of ancient Israel, where terrorism originated. The book called this ancient pattern of events harbingers, and suggested how they've manifested in our modern time.

The pattern of events occurred over a period of seven years. The seven years is a prophetic phase line, and there are three such periods. This is partially where the idea of 7-7-7 comes from, the end result is 21 years, although this isn't articulated in the book. The outcome of this pattern was the fall of ancient Israel. Israel did establish nationhood following the Babylonian siege by King Nebuchadnezzar. Is it possible these events could reappear in modern time? Is there a biblical pattern and the judgement of a nation? It is said that history repeats itself, but to what degree?

Isaiah was a prophet in the ancient times of Israel's collapse and the fall of Jerusalem. He recorded his interpretation of those events in what we now have as the Bible. He was known as a seer and a man of God in those days. He willingly offered his services to "The Holy one of Israel" as is quoted in the Bible. Like described in the scripture, Isaiah, filled with iniquity, saw the throne of God and was fearful. He cursed himself for being unworthy because he has seen the divine creator. An Angel of God came down and touched his lips with coal, atoning for his sin. He was scarred for life and the people could see he served the Holy God.

The harbingers are nine separate events surrounding Jerusalem and now the modern United States of America. I read the book in a week and cross-referenced the material, fact checking everything. At the same time, with the ideas of this book in my conscious thought, I began to see similar patterns unfold in the news. When I finished reading the book, I could see a pattern in my own story as well. I felt I could relate since I joined the Army after 9/11.

I decided to start reading the Bible. These events intrigued me because they concerned ancient records known as scriptures and those scriptures evolved into what we now have as the King James Bible. I didn't know where to start, so I started flipping through pages aimlessly.

Patterns

I didn't really want to read the Bible but sought answers from what happened to me. I started watching videos to grasp the concept of the story. I read *Harbinger* in March and began watching sermons about biblical events and God's word in April. At the same time, the first Blood Moon appeared on April 14, 2014. NASA stated there was a series of blood moons and a solar eclipse called a tetrad would appear on God's Holy Feast days depicted in the book of Leviticus, Chapter 23. I thought I recognized another pattern that grasped my attention. As time has unfolded, the Blood Moons actually have appeared on Biblical Feast Days during the crucifixion. Those signs are written in the book of Joel 2:31 and Acts 2:20. The same blood moon pattern is now under way, and it all coincides with prophesy regarding Israel's birth as a nation and the great and terrible day of the Lord.

Throughout May and all of June, I started to understand the law and nature of sin. I began asking questions to the people making sermons. While asking questions to one of the video makers, a man named Glenn told me to stop asking him questions. Glenn said, "Just read the Bible!" I knew instantly after months of searching he had a point. I thought he was right, but I still didn't know where to start. At this point a new organization swept across the Middle East known as ISIS. This group of Islamic Jihadist swept across Syria and Iraq, barbarically cutting the heads of Christians in the region. This is actually referenced in biblical scripture. Revelation 6:9 describes those Christians who are slain due to the faith.

I again found myself looking through the pages for a starting point. I noticed my name was in the Bible and that there were two letters addressed to Timothy written by the Apostle Paul. I looked at the writing style and thought it would be a challenge. Months prior, after listening to many sermons, I remembered someone saying to pray before reading, so I prayed out loud, "God, help me out and open my heart and eyes." I was asking him to help me understand. I started the Second Letter to Timothy because it was the shorter than the first. I supposed it would have everything the first letter left out and it would be better. On closer inspection, I took notice of the verse numbers and then thought about my call sign as a Paratrooper in the 82nd Airborne. The call sign I had was "Delta 23." That is second platoon, third section. That is where I learned the mentality of a Paratrooper and to never quit. I went to my call sign in the Bible to see what it said first. I was surprised, 2 Timothy 2:3 says, *Thou, therefore, endure hardness, as a good soldier of Jesus Christ.*

After never achieving my military goals, fighting through multiple deployments, injury, facing traumatic amputations, medication addiction and suicide, I clearly had endured seven hardships as a good soldier. Those words written two thousand years ago resonated with me in a way beyond my comprehension. I was shocked; I knew I was onto something, and this was just the beginning. I decided I was on the right path and began reading the New Testament, which introduced the life of Jesus Christ, he was prophesized throughout the Old Testament. I started reading Matthew which is the beginning of the New Testament. It starts off with the genealogy of Jesus and how he came from the blood line of King David, the one who killed Goliath of the Philistines. Jesus was born of a virgin woman being separated from inheriting sin due to Adam's sin in the Garden of Eden. All of Adams offspring would be born in sin, but Jesus was born of the Holy Ghost and a virgin, he wasn't born of sin. 1 Corinthians 15:21 reads: *For since by man came death, by man came also the resurrection of the dead.* Jesus grew up serving the God living a Holy life and he started his ministry at 30 years old. He was baptized by John the Baptist in the Jordan River and stated to him that they would complete all righteousness. After the baptism, He first called for the repentance of all sin and to live according to every word that proceeds out of the mouth of God. He fasted for forty days resisting the temptations of Satan. Satan, as current ruler of Earth, tried bribing Christ, offering all the Kingdoms and the glory of nations to him, if he would just worship him. Jesus was tempted three times and resisted Satan. Jesus went on choosing twelve disciples who came from all parts of life. Some were fishermen, another a tax collector, and other common men. He chose them to be fishers of men and to teach the way to God's salvation and the mysteries of God. Jesus performed many miracles, healing thousands. The news of his miracles swept across the nation as thousand came to listen and be healed. As being foretold in the Old Testament Jesus was appointed to death, but at the time the people believed he was going to deliver them from the hands of their oppression.

After three years of ministry, Jesus was betrayed by one of his own disciples Judas Iscariot for 30 pieces of silver by the high priest. They were threatened by Jesus as he moved the crowd when he over turned the money tables in the temple. They were threatened by his knowledge and his claims of being the Son of God. They hatched the plan to kill him, as he was betrayed, Jesus foretold all these things even his own death on the feast of unleavened bread also known as the last supper. While with his disciples and that evening he was betrayed, he told Judas to do what he had to quickly. The following day was the Passover. Jesus Christ foretold that he would be Gods atonement for all sins past present and future and that his death would atonement on the Passover fulfilling prophesy.

Being on the Passover "The Fifth Perfect" Pontius Pilate a title under Emperor Tiberius over Rome, ruled over Judea. One prisoner would be allowed to be released as tradition and there were only two on this Passover, one being Jesus which his name is interpreted as "Safety" and then there was Barabbbas who caused insurrection among the people and charged as a murderer. Barabbas, his name is interpreted as

"Son of the Father." Pilate would release one prisoner and the people chose Barabbas over Jesus who was accused of Blasphemy. But the spiritual significance of their names and Jesus's work means *"Safety through Son of the Father"* That's a spiritual meaning how there is safety through Son of the Father in Heaven, through Christ, Gods mediator. The bible is full of spiritual meaning and signs.

He was scourged and then led to Golgotha which is a place being interpreted as a skull accompanied with his cross. On the way because he was beaten so badly was exhausted, a certain man was ordered by the Romans to help Jesus carry the cross the rest of the way. Once at Golgotha, Jesus was nailed and raised on the cross in the morning of the Passover which was fulfilling prophesy, which also can be found in Exodus. Similar to the Hebrew's were delivered from the hand of Pharaoh, and therefore, their first born was saved by the blood of the lamb on the Passover. The next day, if the doors weren't cover in lamb's blood as instructed by Moses, then the first born child would be dead. Jesus was the Lamb of God and with his blood and teachings all were in safety. At the Last Supper, he stated if we drink this wine, representing his blood, and eat of his body so then we absorb his ways. He was the Lamb of God declared not just by John the Baptist, but also the Angel Gabriel declared this to Mary in Luke 1:26-38:

> [26]And in the sixth month the angel Gabriel was sent from God unto a city of Galilee, named Nazareth,
>
> [27]To a virgin espoused to a man whose name was Joseph, of the house of David; and the virgin's name was Mary.
>
> [28]And the angel came in unto her, and said, Hail, thou that art highly favored, the Lord is with thee: blessed art thou among women.

²⁹ And when she saw him, she was troubled at his saying, and cast in her mind what manner of salutation this should be.

³⁰ And the angel said unto her, Fear not, Mary: for thou hast found favor with God.

³¹ And, behold, thou shalt conceive in thy womb, and bring forth a son, and shalt call his name Jesus.

³² He shall be great, and shall be called the Son of the Highest: and the Lord God shall give unto him the throne of his father David:

³³ And he shall reign over the house of Jacob forever; and of his kingdom there shall be no end.

³⁴ Then said Mary unto the angel, How shall this be, seeing I know not a man?

³⁵ And the angel answered and said unto her, The Holy Ghost shall come upon thee, and the power of the Highest shall overshadow thee: therefore also that holy thing which shall be born of thee shall be called the Son of God.

³⁶ And, behold, thy cousin Elisabeth, she hath also conceived a son in her old age: and this is the sixth month with her, who was called barren.

³⁷ For with God nothing shall be impossible.

³⁸ And Mary said, Behold the handmaid of the Lord; be it unto me according to thy word. And the angel departed from her.

Just as it was written in Isaiah 53, he was beaten for our transgressions and the iniquity of us. All was laid on him and by his stripes we are healed. One of the most amazing things is that 500 years prior to these events, Daniel a eunuch in Babylon, wrote when Jesus would come, which happened 500 years later. And at the timing of his birth the ruler Herod sought to destroy all the children of Israel, for fear of the coming of the Just One.

After reading through Matthew, I reached Chapter 26, Verse 52. The context of the verse states that "all who pick up the sword and live by the sword will perish by it." When I read the verse, I instantly thought how I heard those words the instant killing the Taliban fighter. "Live by the sword, die by the sword" is what I heard and it was Gods voice.

I finished Matthew, and it ends with Jesus being resurrected from the dead on the third day, conquering death, known as "First Fruits." The Feast days are written in Leviticus chapter 23 as a dress rehearsal for the people to pay attention every year for the coming of Jesus. With his coming it would put an end to the animal sacrifice because he was the perfect sacrifice which needs no other. Because of his righteousness, death could not hold him, he was perfect and blameless before God and he paved the way for the redemption of our sins. The wages of sin is death and all come short of the glory of God as it's written in Romans 3: 23.

He is the worthy mediator between us and the Holy Creator. He renews our heart and mind by baptizing with the Holy Ghost after true repentance and humbleness before his presence. First fruits means giving thanks to God and an offering a tithe for the sacrifices made and the repentance of sin. Jesus commanded his disciples as he was changed with a glorified body to "teach all others baptizing in the name of the Son, the Father and the Holy Ghost." He said that "he would be with them always, even until the end of the world, Amen."

The disciples wanted to know when Jesus would return and the signs of the times. Matthew 24 speaks of prophesy for his second coming and the end of the world. Jesus told them, "I go and prepare a place for you and I will be back. 2 Peter 3:8 says, "But, beloved, be not ignorant of this one thing, that one day *is* with the Lord as a thousand years, and a thousand years as one day," with that being said Jesus said he will come quickly and his second coming is even at the door step. Could it take a day to get to Heaven and a day to get back? To Jesus it would be two days, but to us on Earth, two thousand years. Even Israel was off the map for 2,000 years. Right before Israel became a nation again, May 14, 1948, the year prior the Dead Sea scrolls where recovered, revealing a copy of the book Isaiah perfectly persevered. When compared to modern translations, it was word for word perfectly preserved. God preserved his word as stated in Matthew 24:35: *Heaven and earth shall pass away, but my words shall not pass away.* All the ancient knowledge has been destroyed and lost throughout all the ages, civilizations have come and gone, but the scriptures of God and his work on his people will be fulfilled and endures, but I am really getting a head of myself, but I'm passionate about what I've come to believe.

Reading Mark, I came upon Chapter 9, Verse 45, it pertains to the teachings of Jesus, speaking on hell and sins: "And if thy foot offend thee, cut it off: it is better for thee to enter halt into life, than having two feet to be cast into hell, into the fire that never shall be quenched." This reminded me of my bargaining with God in Afghanistan: "Take both my legs, I'll read your word and spread your word." Then I was attacked and blown up on the next patrol. I could see the connection between how I broke God's commandment and was convicted by the Holy Spirit and how I bargained to serve him in exchange for my life and legs. I had no idea the bible had knowledge like this, and how it is applied in today's world. I was thinking it was kind of like Karma. Karma makes no sense to me anymore, the scripture is like a truth hammered into me. I could see how the values I lived by were

Godly and how the United States Army constructed its values based on faith from over 200 years ago. I quickly started living those values for Jesus, as I was now out of the Army. George Washington even stated: "It is every person's responsibility to be a good Christian Soldier." I lived the Army values for the Army, giving them 100% of who I was, but now I'm giving it to Jesus 100%. He says in Matthew 23:11, "The greatest among you will be your servant." As I served the people of the United States and lived the Army values, I do it now for Jesus Christ because of his sacrifice on the cross and the gift of the Holy Ghost and the people deserve to be notified.

After reading and finishing Luke, I was thinking about the signs in the heaven in Chapter 21:25: *And there shall be signs in the sun, and in the moon, and in the stars; and upon the earth distress of nations, with perplexity; the sea and the waves roaring,* which is also up in the sky and space. The tsunami that took out the Fukushima power plant has been spilling radiation into the Pacific Ocean since March 2011. Also in the same year, I saw the beam of light shooting across the sky I never seen before. Is it possible these are the signs of the time prophesied? Revelation 8:6 speaks of a third of the marine life will die and the ships will be destroyed. It will look like the Pacific Ocean is the prime candidate, being a third part of the waters on Earth.

I started reading the Gospel according to John. In Chapter 15:13, Jesus had said, "Greater love hath no man than this, that a man lay down his life for his friends." I thought instantly how I made my first prayer before deployment. I said "God, if you're really out there and someone has to go, then just take me instead of my men." I started thinking that I been chosen and found favor in God, and at the time I didn't even know existed. I offered myself as a sacrifice on my men's behalf and that type of mentality wins battles, fighting for your men from unspoken brotherhood of loyalty. I didn't realize that God honors sacrifices as he sacrificed his son on the cross. I was thankful for the sacrifice and knowledge that saves us through faith as articulated in 1 Corinthians 15: 1-4.

The Resurrection of Christ

1 Corinthians 15:1-4: *Now, brothers and sisters, I want to remind you of the gospel I preached to you, which you received and on which you have taken your stand. (2) By this gospel you are saved, if you hold firmly to the word I preached to you. Otherwise, you have believed in vain. (3) For what I received I passed on to you as of first importance: that Christ died for our sins according to the Scriptures, (4) that he was buried, that he was raised on the third day according to the Scriptures,*

I began to see a significant pattern based what happened to me in relation to the bible. I was also reading the Old Testament, and had begun the book of Numbers, which was written by Moses. It spoke of the Hebrew fighting strength after the Exodus. Numbers Chapter 1:3 was a personal revelation: *"All who are called to fight in war are the ages of twenty and above."* I was twenty when I first joined the Army. I tried to go earlier, but that couldn't happen. I was too stupid at the time for slacking off in school.

These similarities to my life happened around major events like 9/11 and now retirement. Once I reached Chapter 4:3 in Numbers, I was 31 years old and it completely surprised me, this was like a spiritual adventure coming to all this knowledge. It says *"all who are called to serve God in the host of the tabernacle of the congregation are the ages of thirty and older until the age of fifty years."* Words don't explain how I felt coming to see these patterns. In my twenties, I was serving in a time of war, I then made those prayers inadvertently, enlisting into the service of God or in other words, being called by him. I was astonished and even more than amazed. I could see spiritual connections and how there was another force directing my path throughout my career, even my failures. I was injured during my eighth year of service, and from a biblical point of view, It was like starting a new week or phase. It was the pattern of 7 which stood out. I served for 7 years going into my eighth year in 2011. I was deployed, and after two prayers my men don't get killed and boom everything changed.

I could see all the links to formulate my own personal testimony how Jesus Christ had started changing my life more righteously. I thought that I inadvertently sought favor in his eyes, and that I was chosen to endure such hardships, then it donned on me... the name of my unit, "Chosin!"

Chosin

I was in the 10th Mountain Division, 3rd Brigade 1-32 Infantry "Chosin" Battalion. Our motto was "Against All Odds;" I realized the spiritual connections in every aspect of my life. It was as if I were climbing a spiritual glory, coming full circle. Is it possible that the Lord God was showing me my purpose in life?

Serving the people of the United States and living the Army Values has been the most humbling experience of my life. I am profoundly grateful for everything I have endured in my life. I may have been blown in half, but I have been given a second chance to do what is right. During the time I was learning to have faith in Jesus, I was trying to help guide my wife in the same knowledge. She didn't enjoy listening to me or watching me live a more righteous life-style. She left me with an ultimatum. I was talking to her about what I was learning, and she said to me "Tim, I don't even know you anymore. It's either me or God?" I was completely shocked with my wife's ultimatum and immediately said: "You can't do that." I was praying for months about my marriage and hoped we could reconcile.

I ended up leaving for a few days after to visit my friend Jeremy in South Carolina. I needed some time to breathe and think things over. I found myself at a Barnes and Noble when I saw the Bible section I went over and purchased my first Bible. I went home over the weekend and saw my wife sitting on the couch. I greeted her, showed her what I brought home, and began to tell her that we should get remarried through a church. I showed her the Bible and explained to her how important it was to me. She turned me away and told me I needed to find someone else who would read it with me. I was heartbroken. During the time, I worked out daily and continued praying for guidance. I knew that my relationship was deteriorating, and I prayed and prayed about what to do. I needed a sign and help from God. After a trip to Walter Reed on July 16, I had received an answer to my prayers.

Encounter

After arriving back home from a trip to Walter Reed, I prayed and had a dreamed with an encounter with an Angel disguised as a handicapped man. I was praying for a lot of things at the time. I was watching the emergence of ISIS and the unfolding of other prophesies. I could see financial judgment on the horizon. The spending our nation embarked on will leave us little people in a heap ruin. As you inflate the money the supply the prices go up, but the banks are holding all the money. I had visions of hell and I didn't want to go back and now here I am a legless freak that can't do anything, soon as the economy crashes I'm toast. I was desperate and was always praying for guidance and if Jesus actually knew who I was. The scripture states that there are those at the judgment of God pleading with Jesus that they worked for him casting out devils, but he says he never knew them. I wanted to know if he knew who I was and on the night of July 16th I had received an answer if I was saved.

My wife and I were together in the dream, and we were headed to a party out in the country. It was so vivid, I remember feeling the summer wind while driving in my van with the windows open. When we arrived at the destination – a farm, I parked in a large barn. The barn was full of clutter and after cautiously parking, I pushed the button to open the side door in the van to lower the ramp. Sometimes the ramp would get stuck, and the only thing I could do was to push the ramp lightly. It was stuck; so I asked her to pull the ramp down. She angrily replied, "Fine." As she exited the van, she pulled the ramp and broke it into pieces .I said to her "All you had to do was pull it down." She told me that I had to deal with it. With no choice, I rolled out of the van on the broken ramp and told her "You broke this, you fix it. They're waiting for us."

I left her in the barn with the clutter and went into the massive house adjacent to let everyone know we arrived.

Once inside, I discovered it was empty because all of the guests were out back on the deck. I rolled to the back door, and after sliding the door open, I realized I had legs again and then began walking. I stepped out onto the massive deck and noticed the guests sitting in hot tubs on the far side. I made my way closer to them.

There was one guest who was not in the hot tub, and I noticed he had a disability. His arms were incredibly short, but the rest of his body was proportional. I approached the gentleman and saw one of the guests look up from the hot tub to the right. There were three hot tubs and each were full of people, but this person to the right looked familiar. No one else looked familiar to me. He was my friend's Dad that passed away five years before in March. He spoke to aloud, saying: "Who will help this man?" I raised my hand to help replying "I will."

I approached the man and kneeled down to him. I ask him what he needed while his eyes were fixated toward the floor. He looked at me and said, "Do you know what's going to happen?" I replied without thinking, "Yes. The end of the world, but I don't know how." He said, "There will be three man-made disasters and four natural disasters." I replied, "Okay." And then he said, "When you see the four figs fall from the fig tree then you will know." Confused, I responded immediately, "What?" While I was replying to him, he lifted his small arm to my face and tapped me on the chin. As soon as he touched my chin, he said I was blessed.

In that instant, I could feel myself ascending upward, weightless and flying toward the sky. An overwhelming sense peace and joy rushed through me followed by a pulsating light of explosion that emanated through my body. With that flash of pure white light, I woke up from my dream feeling weightless as if I were just on a rollercoaster ride. I knew this was the sign I prayed for, and I could feel the baptism of

Jesus's Holy Spirit as he promised us. I thought about what I need to do, and decided to write it down. I realized I had this dream exactly three years after waking up in the hospital two weeks after the attack experiencing two weeks in hell, heaven, and nuclear war. This was a pattern of three, and it being three years later was astonishing to think about Gods timing. This was the healing of the mind, body and finally the spirit.

Parallels

My wife and I had been spiritual divided for months, and I couldn't handle the division anymore. I ended our marriage by telling her to leave our apartment the same day I was baptized August 2, 2014. At the same time, as I repented for my sins, I was contacting the people I sinned against to seek their forgiveness. The scripture states to be humble, and if you do something against another then seek forgiveness from them. I called ex-girlfriends, and a particular person who I always cared for and loved came back in my life. When serving God, it's a package deal. He paves the way through tribulation, and now things seemed to brightening up for me. She told me she would be there for me as she was at the hospital for weeks after injury. I was grateful to her.

At that point, my divorce attorney had prepared the necessary divorce documents to be filed and he called me on

9/11. Wow, I thought. I signed the papers on 9/11, which I thought couldn't be a coincidence since I joined the Army because of 9/11. The papers were filled, and just two months later it would be finalized, this time on Veterans Day, which reminded me just two years prior when I encountered the presence of the Holy Spirit and heard the voice "Get off all the medications, its killing you!" That was the second I took a puff of marijuana and realized how bad all the medications were. The divorce was ruled as no fault, originally we wanted to file for an annulment but knew it would have taken much longer.

After that dream is when I first started writing the events of my testimony that are linked to the Bible. I was so shocked with some of the actions I had taken and as a result am now more zealous to serve Jesus. Peter, a disciple of Jesus, wanted to fight for Christ and save him from capture. He said he would even die for him. Before Jesus was captured at Gethsemane, Jesus spent all night praying to God the Father in Heaven, asking if it was possible to escape his fate, but instantly submitting to his Father's will. Christ told Peter he would deny him three times that night, then the rooster would crow. After Jesus was taken into captivity, by the betrayal of Judas the disciples scattered like sheep fulfilling prophecy Zachariah 13:7 *"Awake, O sword, against my shepherd, and against the man that is my fellow, saith the LORD of hosts: smite the shepherd, and the sheep shall be scattered: and I will turn mine hand upon the little ones."* All the disciples scattered and Peter was accused of being a follower of Christ, he denied the accusation and then fled. A second time he was spotted and accused of following Jesus, but he denied a second time giving an oath and a rooster crowed as he departed. The third time he was spotted and accused by a maiden of the Chief Priest, he cursed the multitudes and declared he knew not what they spoke of, then immediately rooster crowed. He recalled the words of Jesus said to him and realized he denied him like Jesus said he would. He held his head down low and left weeping.

After reading about Peter, I realized I denied Christ three times as well. Once after being injured, the second time during the medication addiction, and the third from suicide. He helped me through each of the events and I never gave him credit for helping me. It was like the 10 lepers Jesus healed only one turned back to give thanks. After realizing the connections, I began seeing how I needed to go out and share the testimony of how Jesus intervened in my path and there were a lot of parallels and a flip side to everything endured.

While Jesus was praying all night long, he was betrayed by Judas Iscariot, captured, and then brought before the high priest, Pontus Pilate, for trial. He was executed on the Passover Feast fulfilling the prophecy. The parallel I see is that I prayed all night long bargaining with God to take my legs in exchange for my life and to serve to him. On the third day of July, it happened. The timing isn't coincidental. Even in the book of Leviticus, Chapter 16, and the book of

Genesis, God says all sin has the penalty of death, Although Jesus puts an end to the sacrifice the slaying of the goat I witnessed the day prior to my attack is symbolic of the Old Testament and how all sin needs to be atoned for.

Throughout the Old Testament, Israel would always sacrifice a goat being the escape goat for their sins committed against God. It was a dress rehearsal preparing for the coming of Jesus as God promised and foretold. He would provide the sacrifice on our behalf, that way we could be saved and that's why Jesus came in the first place God would come in the form of man to die as penalty of sin but because he was perfect death could not kill him and all authority in heaven and on Earth was given to him upon his resurrection. He holds the keys to life and death. The Goat I watched get slaughtered July 2, 2011 was symbolic to biblical custom of atoning for sin and I saw a connection there. I filmed the slaying, after which I was selected for the last patrol and was attacked. It was confirmation my bargain was underway.

I was on the show "Two Weeks in Hell" on the Discovery Channel, training for Special Forces. It foreshadowed what was coming. Spending two weeks in a medicated coma was a fight for my life, and after expiring many times, I descended to the depths of She'ol which most would call hell. (She'ol, in the Hebrew Bible, is a place of darkness to where all the dead go, both the righteous and the unrighteous, regardless of the moral choices made in life, a place of stillness and darkness cut off from life.) And then ascending up toward the heavens and witnessing preparation for a massive war like what is written in Revelation Chapter 12:7-12. I wanted to stay and fight, but I was told I had to fulfill my bargain. On the way back, I glimpsed nuclear war in China, seeing their flags and atomic bombs exploding throughout the nation. Passing through the war, I suddenly woke up. It was two weeks after injury, and now fully conscience my first words to my Dad were: "Nuclear was is no good." Everything since then was a fight to get to where I am now.

I tried out for Special Operation four times, and Jesus spoke to me on this matter and asked me why I was so blind. I realized I tried out for Rangers and was injured. I was sent to the 82nd Airborne Division "Americas Guard of Honor," and then after I signed up for Special Forces Assessment and Selection, I received orders for Army recruiting. Recruiting is to strengthen the ranks of the Army. The third time I tried for selection, I got injured during "Two Weeks in Hell" and moved to personnel recovery operations. Personnel Recovery operations retrieves lost people. The fourth time I was submitting an application for covert civil affairs, but before going to school I deployed. On deployment I was attacked and lost my legs in the "The Devils Playground."

Jesus said, "Don't you see how I kept you safe? Or what I've done? You almost got yourself killed? I gave you orders to defend Americas honor because you're recruiting for me now. This is a personnel recovery operation, and I need you in civil affairs. If you want to be special don't be special for yourself, go and be special for me and I will take you to heaven. Tell everyone how I saved you and how I can save them."

My reply to Jesus Christ was a simple, "Roger that!" I published my first book, "The Squad Leaders Bargain" on September 22, 2014. NASCAR was right around the corner and I had intentions to donate the story to the race car drivers. My Nana just passed away, so I figured this would be a great way to honor her memory by giving my story to the racers. Now I had to think of a way to honor my other Grandmothers memory because she just passed away the year prior. I called my mom after publishing my book and she said to her on September 22 "Aren't you proud of your son? I published my book today?" She said, "Of course I am and you know what? Today is Grandmas birthday." I was blown away that God provided a way. I was going to do something later for her but the Holy Spirit woke me up early on the 22nd ordering me to publish the book. I had multiple places to go now that I finished. The first stop is Fort Drum, I called my special friend and said I'd be back in a week. I was going to Fort Drum because I was Chosin! To be continued...

After Thoughts

We're headed into deep territory in our nation and around the world. There are is prophesy that warns us of Gods great judgement coming upon the Earth. We live in this fallen world destroyed by sin. 75% of the Bible is prophecy and 85% of those prophesies have come to pass, the remaining events are surrounded by Gods judgment, the second coming of Christ, his 1000 year Millennial Kingdom and then the New Heaven and a New Earth after Satan, the fallen angels, death and all other not found in the lambs book of life will be cast into the lake of fire. The lake of fire is the second death. Fear not one who can destroy the body but fear God who can destroy the body and the soul. Repent in the name of Jesus and believe he died on the cross for your sins was buried for three days and resurrected on the third and all who call upon the name of the Lord shall be saved. May the Lord be with you.

Made in the USA
Columbia, SC
09 June 2017